THE TREASURES OF ST PAUL

Alan Robinson

The treasures of St Paul

Selected themes from
Paul's theology and ethics

ST PAULS

Cover design by Mary Lou Winters fsp

ST PAULS
Middlegreen, Slough SL3 6BT, United Kingdom
Moyglare Road, Maynooth, Co. Kildare, Ireland

© ST PAULS (UK) 1995

ISBN 085439 500 8

Set by TuKan, High Wycombe
Printed by Biddles Ltd, Guildford

ST PAULS is an activity of the priests and brothers of the Society of St Paul who proclaim the Gospel through the media of social communication

Contents

Introduction

The aim of this book is to explore St Paul's thinking, mainly as expressed in his letters, but with occasional reference to Acts of the Apostles. His writings contain many treasures of theological thought and much wise advice about Christian ethics. Paul's ideas are dealt with thematically, with selections from the letters attributed to him, that is, those from Romans through to Philemon. Each passage is explored in its context and an attempt is made to suggest modern parallels to the situations Paul is writing about.

Paul did not set out to write a systematic theology or to produce an ethical code. Indeed, his letters were written at different times for different purposes. Nevertheless, it is worthwhile grouping thematically ideas expressed by Paul in his letters in order to illustrate patterns in his thinking. When this is done there is an evident unity in Paul's ideas about God and about human relationships. This is not surprising because, after all, the letters all arise from the same source. It would be unwise to argue that because the letters differ in style they were not written or inspired by Paul. Genius is not to be confined by a particular form or style.

For those who are not familiar with the apostle's life and work, it may be helpful to say that he was converted from being a persecutor of the early Christians to becoming a Christian himself. His special conversion experience while he was travelling to Damascus is described in Acts of the Apostles, a biblical book in which Paul is one of the main characters. After his conversion there are thirteen or fourteen mysterious years during which he probably worked out his Christian theology. Then he became a missionary and travelled widely throughout the Roman empire in order to bring people to faith in Christ. Eventually he was martyred for the faith he had striven so indefatigably to spread. The main sources for our knowledge about St Paul are his own letters and Acts of the Apostles.

Paul was chosen by God to be the main spiritual architect of the early Church. He was admirably qualified for this vocation because he was not only an educated Jew, but he was also a Roman citizen and, as he was born and bred in Cilicia (an area steeped in Greek culture), he had a knowledge of Greek thought. On the one hand, his knowledge of Judaism enabled him to understand the meaning of Christ's Messiahship and to work out a Christian theology. On the other hand, his cosmopolitan viewpoint made him an ideal missionary to take the gospel to different parts of the Roman Empire.

Thirteen of the twenty seven documents in the New Testament are attributed to St Paul. His writings comprise between a quarter and a third of the New Testament. These letters were probably written between about 48 and 64 AD, though these dates are disputed. Indeed, some people argue that Paul did not write all of the letters attributed to him. However, early Church tradition is in favour of Pauline authorship. Letters which have been seriously challenged on the question of authorship include, for example, Ephesians, Colossians, II Thessalonians and the Pastoral Letters (i.e. I and II Timothy and Titus). Some scholars argue that some of the letters have been edited by another hand and that at least one has been put together from fragments of shorter letters by Paul. However, all of this is speculation. No one has finally disproved the Pauline authorship of the letters attributed to him. The position taken in this book is that Paul either wrote the letters himself or that his thinking lies behind them.

St Paul's writings have greatly influenced many people, including, for example, St Augustine of Hippo and John Wesley. In the view of many Christians, Paul is the greatest Christian theologian the Church has ever produced. His work is an essential part of the Christian revelation, and as such will continue to influence Christian thinkers in future centuries.

I

Paul introduces himself

Paul, a servant of Jesus Christ, called to be an apostle, set apart for the Gospel of God which he promised beforehand through his prophets in the holy scriptures, the gospel concerning his Son, who was descended from David according to the flesh and designated Son of God in power according to the Spirit of holiness by his resurrection from the dead, Jesus Christ our Lord, through whom we have received grace and apostleship to bring about the obedience of faith for the sake of his name among all the nations, including yourselves who are called to belong to Jesus Christ; To all God's beloved in Rome, who are called to be saints: Grace to you, and peace from God our Father and the Lord Jesus Christ.

(Romans 1:1-7)

This is an amazing opening paragraph for a letter, even one with such serious intentions as that to the congregation at Rome. Paul makes it crystal clear that he is God's special messenger. The word *apostle* (Greek *apostolos*) literally means "one who is sent". This, of course, is reminiscent of the Old Testament prophets who believed they were "sent" by God (see especially Isaiah 6:8). It is also obvious that Paul is stating his credentials as one with authority equal to that of the twelve apostles. It is almost as if he had a chip on his shoulder in this respect, because he had once persecuted the early Christians. But that very "chip" may well have motivated him to aim for excellence in his vocation, and the results of his life's work speak for themselves.

Paul also states his main aim in life with great clarity. He is "set apart for the gospel." This "good news" is about

God's Son. Perhaps the word "gospel" (good news) is something of an understatement. What Paul is bringing is *astounding* news. The Supreme Being, the Creator of all that is, has sent his Son to live upon earth among ordinary people. That is, God has made actual an incarnation of his own Godhead. But that is only part of the astonishing news. Death, the scourge of mankind, has been shown to be a doorway to everlasting life. Moreover, that very resurrection was an authenticating sign of God's power operating through his Son. It is as if the midwife at our birth had become the doorkeeper at our death. Or as if a new sun had risen as the old, familiar sun was setting. This gospel is as astonishing in this century as it was in the first century.

Another quite amazing part of this good news is that it was announced "beforehand through the prophets". There are so many places in the Old Testament where it is possible to perceive with the wisdom of hindsight that God was warning a particular group of people what was to come. Indeed, the equivalent word for "gospel" or "gospel bringer" is used in the Hebrew prophecies of Isaiah:

"How beautiful upon the mountains
are the feet of him who brings good tidings of good,
who publishes peace, who brings good tidings of good,
who publishes salvation,
who says to Zion, 'Your God reigns'" (Isaiah 52:7).

God was indeed going to publish salvation, the potential salvation of the whole world. And then there are those prophecies which write of a coming king with divine authority. For example, Isaiah writes:

"For to us a child is born,
to us a son is given;
and the government will be upon his shoulder,
and his name will be called
'Wonderful Counsellor, Mighty God,
Everlasting Father, Prince of Peace'" (Isaiah 9:6).

Paul was familiar with such prophecies because he knew the Old Testament scriptures more or less off by heart. He had no doubt at all, when he had come to terms with his conversion experience, that God had spoken beforehand of the coming of Jesus Christ.

This wonderful news was not only for the Roman Christians, but also for all nations. Whether Paul knew that his letters would be read for centuries after his death is impossible to say, but the fact is that he was completely convinced that his mission was a universal one. If Paul had not taken this mission seriously, the gospel would not have spread as widely and as quickly as it did throughout the Mediterranean world. Since then, there have been thousands of men and women who have been inspired by St Paul and they have also travelled widely in order to spread the gospel. The followers of St Ignatius Loyola (the Jesuits), for example, had missions all over the world from the sixteenth century onwards. They went to India, Malaya, the Congo, Brazil, Japan, Ethiopia and China. It is similarly the duty of Christians in later generations to follow Paul's example, even if it means one day travelling to other planets.

Paul greets the "saints" in Rome with a prayer for grace and peace to their community. There are several levels of meaning in the Greek word for "saints". Then, of course, there is the growth in the idea in later centuries that the Church has the power to declare that certain men and women are saints in a very particular way. Probably Paul means in this letter that the people of the Roman church have a call to be holy people and that they have been separated from the world by God to be his children. This description may be applied to any Christian congregation, though it may need just a little explanation, the point being that people are "saints" because of what God does for them and not because of what they do for him. As Isaac Watts writes:

"Beneath the shadow of Thy throne,
Thy saints have dwelt secure;
Sufficient is Thine Arm alone,
and our defence is sure."

Bible readings:

- Philippians 3:4-9 (Personal details)
- Acts 9:1-30 (Conversion)

II
What is God like?

1. God is our Father

When we cry, "Abba! Father!" it is the Spirit himself bearing witness with our spirit that we are children of God...

(Romans 8:15b-16)

It is traditional among both Jewish people and Christians to address God as Father. There will be few Christians who are not familiar with the Lord's Prayer, sometimes called the "Our Father". But perhaps not everyone knows that Jews before the time of Jesus addressed God in this way. Jeremiah wrote, for example, speaking for God:

"And I thought you would call me My Father,
and would not turn from following me."

(Jeremiah 3:19)

Nevertheless, Jesus was obviously the first to address the Father in this way because he is and always was the eternal Son. That is why St Paul was able to say, "I bow my knees before the Father, from whom every family in heaven and on earth is named..." (Ephesians 3:14-15). In other words, God was the first Father and Christ was the first Son. Human parenthood is therefore patterned on the Fatherhood of God. That is one aspect of the many faceted idea that we are "made in God's image." That in itself is a wonderful thought. It is also wonderful that each and everyone of us may speak to God directly as Father.

The Aramaic word Abba is generally thought to be a

13

childish and intimate way in which Jewish children addressed their human fathers. Children in many countries have fond ways of speaking to their parents. In English, of course, the equivalent would be "Daddy". This modern equivalent is rarely if ever used of God in public worship today. Most church services keep to the more formal "Father". Some scholars, indeed, argue that Abba means "my Father" and that it is fairly formal. What address different people use in their private prayers would be difficult to say, but one suspects that many might be reluctant to use the word Daddy in personal prayers. Nevertheless, Paul appears to recommend the use of Abba, the ancient equivalent, not only here, but also in his letter to the Galatians:

"And because you are sons, God has sent the Spirit of his Son into our hearts, crying, 'Abba! Father!'"

(Galatians 4:6)

The message for us is clear, both from our Lord's use of the phrase (see Mark 14:36), and from St Paul's use. What we are invited to by the Spirit is a very close personal relationship with God. The Trinity is, in effect, a community of love, and we are invited to link ourselves through Christ's prior Sonship to the source of all love. We are invited to be sons and daughters of God. Paul, of course, goes on to say (in the Romans passage) that we are not only children of God, but also "fellow heirs with Christ". Paul also warns that we may be heirs to Christ's suffering before we can inherit Christ's glory.

It may not be easy for some people to see God as Father. If we have loving parents then we can easily make the connection, but what of children who have been abused by their fathers? It may be very difficult for them to link to God as Father in a very personal way. One way round this difficulty perhaps is to ensure that the Father image is painted graphically with loving illustrations. Jesus himself has given some good hints on how to do this in stories like the Prodigal Son in which the father lovingly forgives and embraces his sinful son. Perhaps the most wonderful illustration lies in the words of our Lord on the cross: "Father, forgive them; for they know not what they do" (Luke 23:34).

To live within the love of the Fatherhood of God is not only to have a wonderful experience; it also means accepting a great responsibility. The poet Rudyard Kipling expressed this very well when he wrote:

> "Father in Heaven who lovest all,
> Oh, help Thy children when they call;
> That they may build from age to age
> An undefiled heritage." (From the Children's Song)

Every Christian has the potential to bring other people into a relationship with God our Father. Every Christian, indeed, is called to pass on the tradition of the faith, that all human beings belong to the family of God.

Bible readings

- Acts of the Apostles 1:1-5 (Waiting for the promise of the Father)
- Ephesians 4:1-6 (One God and Father of us all)

2. God is Creator of all things

The God who made the world and everything in it, being Lord of heaven and earth, does not live in shrines made by man, nor is he served by human hands, as though he needed anything, since he himself gives to all men life and breath and everything.

(Acts of the Apostles 17:24-25)

This passage is from Paul's famous sermon preached at Athens. The setting shows how good a teacher Paul was.

15

He had seen an inscription "To an unknown God" while walking along the street. He made this his starting point and then told his sceptical audience that he had come to explain to them who the "unknown God" was.

Paul knew that the Greeks had a strong poetic tradition and so he decided it would be a good tactic to link his sermon to apt quotations from Greek poets: "In him we live and move and have our being," and "For we are indeed his offspring" (see verse 28). The argument then moves to the idea that such a God could not possibly be represented by objects of gold, silver or stone. This is similar to the argument in the Book of Isaiah when the prophet called Second Isaiah was in a similar situation to Paul's, though in Babylon; that is, surrounded by temples and statues dedicated to numerous imaginary gods (see Isaiah 42:5 and 17).

Because Paul had been brought up in Tarsus, a Greek speaking town, he knew quite a lot about Greek traditions. However, he had also been educated at the feet of Gamaliel in the school for Pharisees (cf. Acts 22:3), and was even more steeped in Jewish traditions. He would be familiar with the descriptions of creation in the early chapters of the Book of Genesis and with some of the wonderful passages in the psalms and prophets about creation. (See, for example, Psalm 104 and Isaiah 40.) Paul knew that the Hebrew poets were inspired by the glories of creation as much as, if not more than, the Greek poets he was quoting.

We, too, can be inspired by the beauties of creation. We don't need to open the works of the great poets like Wordsworth, Dante or Goethe, to feel this, though of course the inspiration of others does help our own inspiration. True inspiration is directly between God and ourselves, or between God's wonderful creation and ourselves. God writes upon the stars and the planets, upon the mountains and the valleys, upon the flowers and the trees, upon the oceans and the rivers, upon the sunshine and the rainbows, upon the clouds and the snowflakes. This is the book that the ancient psalmist read and this is the source of the inspiration of the writer of Genesis. The book of nature can also be our inspiration, if we use the senses God has given to us.

Paul knew well that God's revelation is not confined to the scriptures. God has made it plain for all to see that he is the Creator of the universe in the very things we see and touch each day, and in our very selves. This is why Paul was able to say, before he mentioned the revelation through Christ incarnate, that God "gives to all men life and breath and everything." The sermon at Athens is a wonderful model for preachers. Paul started where his listeners actually were, before introducing them to the new and mind bending fact of Christ's resurrection from the dead.

It is interesting that Paul argues that God does not live in shrines made by men. Does that make church buildings redundant? Certainly, Paul, like the later St Francis and John Wesley, as often as not preached out of doors (see Acts 16:13). However, Paul also speaks of the temple of the body (I Corinthians 3:16-17). This does not mean that he would disapprove of the church buildings used today. At the same time, he might challenge us to see whether we had tried to make the church buildings we use into "prisons" to confine God – which is impossible to do in reality, of course, even though misguided human imagination may attempt it.

It is also important to take Paul's point that God "is not served by human hands". In other words, the Creator of all that is, who holds the universe in the hollow of his palm, does not need us, though he has created us in love. He has also created the universe as a place for us to grow into his love.

Bible readings

– Romans 8:18-25 (Creation waits for the revealing of the sons of God)
– Colossians 1:15-20 (Christ, the first born of all creation)

3. He emptied himself, taking the form of a servant

Have this mind among yourselves, which is yours in Christ Jesus, who, though he was in the form of God, did not count equality with God a thing to be grasped, but emptied himself, taking the form of a servant, being born in the likeness of men. And being found in human form he humbled himself and became obedient unto death, even death on a cross. Therefore God has highly exalted him and bestowed on him the name which is above every name, that at the name of Jesus every knee should bow, in heaven and on earth and under the earth, and every tongue confess that Jesus Christ is Lord, to the glory of God the Father.

(Philippians 2: 5-11)

The phrase "in the form of God" makes it quite clear that Paul believed Christ was divine. The Greek word Paul uses for "form" (*morphe*) was used by Aristotle to mean the essential form or character of something. This implies that Christ was showing God's essential character in self sacrificial love, or to put it in another way, in self sacrificial service for others. Thus, the nature of Christ's vocation is placed in the context of the Suffering Servant ideal (see Isaiah 53).

Christ is the eternal Son, but during the Incarnation he shed his divine glory in order to show God's word to the world. This revelation has many aspects, but in the context of this saying in Philippians it can be understood that God has given human beings a pattern to live by, a blueprint to follow. Paul writes, "Have this mind among yourselves...". It follows, then, that the vocation to be a Christian is a call to serve both God and our neighbour (in the widest sense). This, of course, reflects our Lord's summary of the law, in that we are required to love both God and our neighbour above all else.

The amazing quality that God shows to us is a never failing and untiring service that he gives unstintingly in love. The very least we can do is to give a similar service in return to the limits of the gifts we have been given. The famous prayer of St Ignatius Loyola expresses this ideal very well:

"Teach us, good Lord, to serve thee as thou deservest, to give and not to count the cost, to fight and not to heed the wounds, to toil and not to seek for rest, to labour and not to ask for any reward, save that of knowing that we do thy will, through Jesus Christ our Lord. Amen."

The prayer of St Richard of Chichester, on a similar theme, has inspired many to follow in the footsteps of our Lord along the path of suffering love:

"Thanks be to thee, O Lord Jesus Christ, for all the benefits which thou hast given us, for all the pains and insults which thou hast borne for us. O most merciful Redeemer, friend and brother, may we know thee more clearly, love thee more dearly, and follow thee more nearly, now and for ever more. Amen."

We ought not to be discouraged by the wonderful achievements of the great saints, thinking that we can never be anything like them. Every little act of service we do for others is part of the love of Christ. In any case, we do not know what we might achieve unless we make a beginning, even if it is in the most modest way. Some of the greatest saints have been very ordinary people, but the power of the Holy Spirit within them has made them extraordinary. The original apostles provide a good example. The first four people called by Jesus were simple fishermen, but they had the capacity to become great missionaries and great church leaders. If they had not answered God's call through Christ they might never have discovered their hidden talents. Every single human being has the capacity to grow and if this capacity is harnessed to the will of God, then the possibilities are infinite.

As Paul points out in the passage under discussion,

Christ was obedient to death itself; and that death involved an ignominious and painful nailing to a cross. But the results of that action and that self sacrifice are measureless. One obvious result, though, as Paul explains, is "that at the name of Jesus every knee should bow", and "every tongue confess that Jesus Christ is Lord..." This is surely a conscious reference by Paul to a text in the Book of Isaiah:

"To me every knee shall bow,
every tongue shall swear" (Isaiah 45:23).

Isaiah also says in the same verse, "...from my (God's) mouth has gone forth in righteousness a word that shall not return." This is a wonderful example of how the prophecies of the Old Testament are fulfilled in a very particular way. God was and is in Christ and the whole of creation is under his Kingship. If, then, the King of heaven and earth has shown himself to be our servant, it is appropriate that we should also become his servants. Paul certainly felt this very strongly:

"For what we preach is not ourselves, but Jesus Christ as Lord, with ourselves as your servants for Jesus' sake."
(II Corinthians 4:5)

Bible readings

– II Corinthians 11:16-29 (Paul as a suffering servant)
– Acts 16:19-34 (Paul in prison at Philippi)

4. God is faithful

God is faithful, by whom you were called into the fellowship of his Son, Jesus Christ our Lord.
(I Corinthians 1:9)

It may seem unnecessary to say that God is faithful because we would not expect him to be anything else. However, Paul makes this affirmation several times in his letters (cf. I Corinthians 10:13; II Corinthians 1:18; I Thessalonians 5:24). It is as if some of the people of God needed reassurance and, to be sure, most of us at times need some kind of confirmation that God's promises are true and faithful. When life seems dark and the way uncertain it is helpful to have someone like Paul saying us, "Don't worry, God is faithful. He won't let you down."

This is not just whistling in the dark. For thousands of years God has shown himself by sure signs to a whole host of people who have been inspired to trust in his word. Almost three thousand years ago a poet wrote:

"Thy faithfulness endures to all generations;
thou hast established the earth, and it stands fast."

(Psalm 119:90)

Another psalmist wrote:

"I love thee, O Lord, my strength.
The Lord is my rock, and my fortress..."

(Psalm 18:1-2)

King Solomon believed that God would be faithful to the covenant he had made with the house of David:

"O Lord, God of Israel, there is no God like thee,
in heaven above or on earth beneath,
keeping covenant and showing steadfast love
to thy servants who walk before thee ...!"

(I Kings 8:23)

If we accept God as our rock and, if we walk before him, then God will show to us the unchanging faithfulness he has shown to those in the fellowship of the old covenant and to those in the fellowship of the new covenant with

Christ. Paul uses an interesting word when he mentions the "fellowship". The Greek word (*koinonia*) is sometimes translated "communion". When Paul is commenting on the Eucharist he uses this same word. The people have "communion in the blood of Christ" and "communion in the body of Christ" (see I Corinthians 10:16). Paul also writes about the "fellowship of the Holy Spirit" in the famous prayer for grace (II Corinthians 13:14). So in this communion all of us are invited to participate in fellowship with the Lord.

The Church is sometimes referred to as the family of God. All Christians are brothers or sisters in this family. Within any family love and trust normally prevail. In God's family this is even more the case. God is absolutely faithful, so we can place our absolute trust in him. To live each hour of each day in this fellowship with our Lord is a wonderful gift indeed. It means that he is with us in our suffering as well as in our joys. We can take our problems and burdens to him in the full knowledge that he will help us with them. St Paul himself had some very testing experiences. He was shipwrecked, put in gaol, stoned, flogged and finally executed – but he never faltered in his faith in God because he knew that God would never falter in his support. Similarly, in more modern times, Dietrich Bonhoeffer was imprisoned for his faith during the Second World War. His faith, too, remained strong, even to the time of his cruel execution. His writings are his legacy to us and many of his words are truly inspiring. Of the Christian fellowship he wrote:

"In the fellowship of the crucified and glorified body of Christ we participate in his suffering and glory."
(*The Cost of Discipleship*, S.C.M., 1959, p. 219)

Dietrich Bonhoeffer was strong in his faith despite his suffering: he knew in his deepest heart that the God who has called us into the fellowship of Christ is ever faithful.

Bible readings

– Acts 27:21-26 (Paul's faith is shown in adversity)
– Romans 16:25-27 (The obedience of faith)

5. God has eternal power

Ever since the creation of the world his invisible nature, namely, his eternal power and deity, has been clearly perceived in the things that have been made.

(Romans 1:20)

Although God cannot be seen in the same way as your kitchen table, nevertheless his existence can be surmised from the nature of the universe. Further, if God did indeed create the universe, it stands to reason that he was around before the universe. Paul suggests that two qualities in God's nature may be deduced from this. Firstly, he is eternal. Secondly, he is the power behind the universe. It is a bit mind boggling for us to try to imagine eternity. A hundred years seems a long time to us. A thousand years perhaps can be understood, though not experienced. But when we try to imagine tens of thousands of years we have some difficulty. Beyond that we are in the realm of mystery and so the idea of eternity is buried beneath layers and layers of millennia after millennia. Of course, time for God or time in heaven may be different from time as we know it. Many poets have tried to capture something of the mystery of time. The hymn by Isaac Watts is very expressive:

"Time, like an ever-rolling stream,
Bears all its sons away;
They fly forgotten as a dream
Dies at the opening day."

However, time's sons are only forgotten in the realm of time. God's mind may hold them for eternity. In other

23

words, the idea of heaven is within God, just as the idea of the universe is within God. Consequently, the change from earth to heaven for a soul is merely a switch from one idea to another in the eternal mind of God.

One of the most important ways in which the New Testament writers perceived God's power was in the work of the Holy Spirit. Paul himself mentions "the power of the Holy Spirit" (Romans 15:13). The Book of Acts has so many references to the work of the Holy Spirit that it is sometimes called the "Gospel of the Holy Spirit (see for example Acts 1:2; 4:8; 11:24 and passim). The Greek word for power lies behind the English word "dynamo" (Greek *dunamis*). The image of the dynamo is a good way to describe the effect of God's power upon a human life. Very many people have found their lives transformed by the power of the Holy Spirit. Indeed, some people have been able to achieve things they would never have thought possible without the power of God behind them. Moses is a good example, though he may not have described God precisely as the Holy Spirit (but see Numbers 11:17). Through the power of the Spirit Moses was able to do what at first seemed impossible, that is, to lead the Israelite slaves out of Egypt.

Of course, our Lord himself said, "...with God all things are possible" (Matthew 19:26). To put this in another way, we often say that God is "omnipotent". The all-powerful God in whom Christians believe can indeed achieve things which are beyond our limited human capabilities. A number of people who have been cured of apparently incurable illnesses after a trip to Lourdes have personal experience of the unstoppable power of God. God, however, does not supply this power on demand, and presumably he has reasons beyond our full comprehension for sometimes using his power in a miraculous way, and sometimes not. At the same time the powers of nature are such that we should not be surprised at the power of the God who created nature. The fearsome strength of the ocean, or of an earthquake, or of a stellar explosion are wonderful indeed.

The strange thing is that the all powerful God of the beginning of creation is also as gentle as a dove. He is the one who came to serve and to sacrifice himself on our behalf. What a contrast with human misuse of power. History is littered with individuals who have crashed their way to dominance over millions of other people. Too often this power has been corrupt. This thought has been expressed neatly in the words:, "Power tends to corrupt and absolute power corrupts absolutely" (attributed to the first Baron Acton). By contrast, God does have absolute power, but he is absolutely incorruptible.

Bible readings

- Romans 6:20-23 (The free gift of eternal life)
- II Corinthians 12:1-10 (God's power is made perfect in weakness)

6. God is righteous

But now the righteousness of God has been manifested apart from law, although the law and the prophets bear witness to it, the righteousness of God through faith in Jesus Christ for all who believe.

(Romans 3:21-22)

Paul is saying here that God's righteousness has been revealed in at least two ways. The first way was at an earlier stage in the divine revelation. This was through the law and the prophets. Although the Ten Commandments of Moses were only part of Jewish law, they were nevertheless the heart of it. There is a very real sense in which the Israelites came to understand something about the righteousness of God through trying to keep these laws. However, they were not always successful in their attempts to be righteous and the prophets often showed them the error of their ways. Amos, for example, explained to the people that God wanted more than a token appearance in the temple:

"Take away from me the noise of your songs;
to the melody of your harps I will not listen.
But let justice roll down like waters,
and righteousness like an ever-flowing stream."
(Amos 5:24)

The righteous God demanded righteousness from his people. Indeed, his holiness will always demand righteousness from anyone who approaches him. The call to follow Christ is a call to seek holiness and righteousness. However, Paul explains that God's righteousness has been shown in a second stage of revelation, in a way which is "apart from law". This way is the path of faith in Jesus Christ. Paul continues the argument in the next chapter by showing that a person can be made righteous through faith in Christ, apart from the law. He uses Abraham as a wonderful example:

"For what does the scripture say? 'Abraham believed God, and it was reckoned to him as righteousness.'"
(Romans 4:3 cf. Genesis 17:1)

Of course, what faith in Christ does is to put us in the appropriate mental and spiritual state to receive God's grace. Only through the gift of grace are we able to approach the throne of God to have our sins forgiven. In other words, Christ's work of atonement is the means through which the penitent receives God's grace. This is formalised in the sacraments of the Church, the sacraments being the usual, though not the only avenue, by which God gives his grace to the faithful.

It must not be forgotten, of course, that our Lord himself said:

"For I tell you, unless your righteousness exceeds that of the scribes and Pharisees, you will never enter the kingdom of heaven" (Matthew 5:20).

It is clear from the gospels that the "righteousness" of the scribes and Pharisees was based on legalism. Jesus surely did not mean that we had to exceed these people in their legalism, but rather that we should be tuned in to the love of God through his grace.

This principle is very much applicable to everyday life. If you try to be perfect in terms of keeping the moral law, you may well be in danger of missing the most important moral insight of all, which is that answering the call of Christ in faith will bring his gifts of love and grace. These gifts will make you righteous in a new way. You will be a new person who can shine with love in the community to which you belong. You will accept your own weaknesses but will rise above them to be a true servant of God.

The psalmist got it right when he wrote:

"He leads me beside still waters;
he restores my soul.
He leads me in paths of righteousness
for his name's sake" (Psalm 23:2-3).

Bible readings

– I Timothy 6:11-12 (Aim at righteousness)
– Philippians 1:9-11 (The fruits of righteousness)

7. God shows both severity and kindness

Note then the kindness and severity of God: severity towards those who have fallen, but God's kindness to you, provided you continue in his kindness; otherwise you too will be cut off.

(Romans 11:22)

While Paul frequently puts an emphasis on God's love and God's grace (cf. I Corinthians 13 and Philippians 4:23), he certainly does not pull his punches in describing God's judgement of human sinfulness (cf. Galatians 6:7-8). In the Romans passage above Paul contrasts God's kindness and God's severity. The words he uses in this passage (or cognate words) are used also of the way people behave towards each other. For example, Paul writes to Corinth:

"I write this while I am away from you, in order that when I come I may not have to be severe in my use of the authority which the Lord has given me..."

(II Corinthians 13:10)

And in writing to Ephesus he instructs the people:

"...away with all malice, and be kind to one another..."

(Ephesians 4:32)

It is difficult to avoid comparisons with human qualities when we are trying to describe God. We can only use the language that we have. In this example used by Paul, however, he seems to be using everyday words deliberately in order to make an impact upon his readers. Many members of the church in Rome would be non-Jews. Paul compares them in the preceding verses to wild olive tree branches which have been grafted onto the original olive tree of Judaism (Romans 11:17-20). Some of the original branches (i.e. Jewish people) have been broken off because they have not believed in Christ as the new stage of God's revelation. Paul makes the point that the newly grafted branches (i.e. the Gentiles) could also be broken off if they fall away from the faith. At the same time, Jewish people could be grafted in again if they accepted the new faith.

This is a warning to the congregation to remain faithful or take the consequences. It is also a warning to all Christians of all times. God will deal severely with any who fall away. Paul puts this very tactfully. He writes, "...provided you continue in his kindness..." you will receive God's kindness. Paul's own character, perhaps, is shown here. His main message is a loving one and he is indeed a very loving person himself; but he does not suffer arrogant sinners gladly. There is the famous passage where he writes to the Corinthians:

> "What do you wish? Shall I come to you with a rod, or with love in a spirit of gentleness?"
>
> (I Corinthians 4:21)

Any true relationship with God has to take account of the opposing qualities mentioned by Paul. God will be severe with us when our behaviour justifies severity. On the other hand, provided we are living in God's love and consciously trying to practise kindness and love to others, God will show us his kindly grace. It is much better, of course, if we are severe with ourselves and certainly no one could ever say that Paul was ever soft in his own self discipline.

Bible readings

– Acts 13:44-end (Paul's message is rejected by the Jews of Antioch)
– Ephesians 2:10 (God's gracious kindness)

8. God's ways are inscrutable

O the depth of the riches and wisdom and knowledge of God! How unsearchable are his judgements and how inscrutable his ways!
> *"For who has known the mind of the Lord,*
> *or who has been his counsellor?"*
> *"Or who has given a gift to him*
> *that he might be repaid?"*

29

For from him and through him and to him are all things. To him be glory for ever. Amen.

(Romans 11:33-36)

It was Thomas à Kempis who first wrote, "Man proposes but God disposes" (Imitation of Christ). In other words, we sometimes think we know what we are going to do, but events often enough prove us wrong. This is sometimes the case even when we are seeking God's will for us. We may believe we have pierced this mystery, but God then takes us by the ears and places us somewhere else. More than two thousand years before Thomas à Kempis lived, Moses told the people that he had not been able to see God's face, but only his back (Exodus 33:21-23). Here then we have two of the world's greatest religious thinkers, men who had lived close to God, who both testified to God's mysterious and inscrutable ways.

Very gifted people are able to express some of this mystery through words or music, or through a combination of the two. The poet and hymn writer, William Cowper, for example, wrote the beautiful and unforgettable words:

> "God moves in a mysterious way
> His wonders to perform;
> He plants his footsteps in the sea,
> And rides upon the storm."

In the text under discussion, Paul is quoting from two Old Testament books in order to make his point about God's inscrutability (see Isaiah 40:13-14 and Job 35:7, 41:11). The line from Isaiah seems to be one of his favourite quotations because he refers to the same line in his first letter to the Corinthians (2:16). The second Isaiah wrote:

> "Who has directed the Spirit of the Lord,
> or as his counsellor has instructed him?"

(Isaiah 40:13)

Even our Lord himself is quoted in John's Gospel as saying:

"The wind blows where it wills, and you hear the sound of it, but you do not know whence it comes or whither it goes; so it is with every one who is born of the Spirit."
(John 3:8)

The Holy Spirit has a strange way of seeming to let things slide for a time, or even not to be interested in our prayers. Then quite amazingly, when everything is in place, the Holy Spirit acts and our prayers are answered. For example, the foundress of a Catholic order of nuns called the Presentation Sisters prayed for helpers in her teaching work and her work in helping the poor in Ireland in the late eighteenth century. During Nano Nagle's life time she had only a small handful of helpers who became her sisters in the religious way of life. Now, in the twentieth century, Nano's prayers have been answered in the most wonderful way, because thousands of her Sisters the world over are teaching the Christian message and helping the poor.

The mystery of God challenges our worship and our service in Christ. In worship we use many symbols to make our approach to God, some of them, in fact, revealed to us through the Holy Spirit. The water of baptism, the bread and wine of the Eucharist and readings from the Bible are examples of media through which we know God is speaking to us. At the same time, it would be a mistake to conclude that we held God's entire revelation within those media. God is over and beyond anything we can imagine or reason. As Jesus himself said:

"You did not choose me, but I chose you..."
(John 15:16)

Moses was face to face with the mystery of God when he knelt before the burning bush. In the same way, St Paul was dazzled and temporarily blinded by a revelation of

God's mystery while on his way to Damascus. Those whom God has called in a special way are perhaps privileged to perceive more of this mystery than the average person, but nevertheless, every single human being is called to explore a relationship with Almighty God, and in this exploration may be privileged to receive a vision of some aspect of the ultimate mystery. You don't have to be in a particular place to do this. The vision glorious may appear at the doorstep of your own house. When St Ignatius Loyola said, "I can find God wherever I will," presumably he meant that wherever a man or woman is when he or she turns to God, God is always there.

Bible readings

– I Corinthians 2 (The wisdom of God)
– Colossians 1:24-29 (The mystery of God)

9. God is holy

And do not grieve the Holy Spirit of God, in whom you were sealed for the day of redemption.

(Ephesians 4:30)

Paul was brought up in a culture where the idea of God's holiness was a very ancient tradition. The Jewish scriptures are steeped with this idea and not only was God himself regarded as holy, but also any object or place associated with God. An area of the temple was set aside as the Holy of Holies and only the high priest was allowed to enter that part of the temple on one occasion in the year, that is, on the day of Atonement (see Leviticus 16:1-10).

One of the most wonderful perceptions of the holiness of God was written by Isaiah in the Thrice Holy (Trisagion):

"Holy, holy, holy is the Lord of hosts;
the whole earth is full of his glory" (Isaiah 6:3).

This beautiful expression of God's holiness is taken up in slightly different words in the Book of Revelation (Revelation 4:8) and in the liturgy used in the Church today. Bishop Heber took up the same theme in his famous hymn:

"Holy, Holy, Holy; Lord God Almighty!
Early in the morning our song shall rise to Thee:
Holy, Holy, Holy! Merciful and Mighty;
God in Three persons, Blessed Trinity!"

Of the Three Persons, it is the Spirit who has had the word Holy attached permanently to his name, though of course, that does not detract from the holiness of the Father and the Son, who are one with the Holy Spirit.

In the New Testament the emphasis is put on the will of God that his people should grow into holiness. Paul appeals to the Romans, for example:

"I appeal to you therefore, brethren, by the mercies of God, to present your bodies as a living sacrifice, holy and acceptable to God, which is your spiritual
        worship" (Romans 12:1).

This appeal is also to us, but if we are going to try to grow in holiness, perhaps we need to understand what we mean by the holiness of God. Unfortunately, the Bible writers do not give a dictionary definition. However, the Hebrew word may have originally meant "separation", which implies that God was a separate being from ourselves and that holy things were to be separated from ordinary things. In the dictionaries of Biblical Greek a similar origin for the idea of holiness is suggested. This does not take us very far. English dictionaries are no more helpful. They tend to give vague synonyms like "sacred" or "worthy of worship". So where does that leave us? It probably leaves us with the arts. Poets, musicians and artists may possibly take us a little nearer to what we mean by the holiness of God. Our perception may need to be emotional as well as intellectual. For example to listen to Bach's St Matthew Passion: or to read Milton's "Hymn on the Morning of Christ's Nativity"; or to gaze at a Michelangelo fresco in the Sistine Chapel – may give to us some perception of the holiness of God. Equally, however, to walk through a desert alone; or to stand under a clear, starry sky; or to be present at the death of a friend – may give to us a similar perception.

Often, however, we associate holiness with purity in the moral sense. Perhaps it is in this area of our development that we feel we have to develop in holiness. After all, Paul does say that we are "sealed for the day of redemption" in the Holy Spirit. However, the righteousness of God and the love of God are not quite the same as his holiness, though they are not separate from it, because God is indivisible. To approach God in partial awareness of his holiness in some of the aspects we have mentioned, may be at the heart of worship. It is when we worship him in the "beauty of holiness" that we are most truly aware of his might, majesty and power and the holy flame of his presence with us.

Bible readings

- I Corinthians 3:16-17 (God's temple is holy)
- Colossians 1:21-23 (Paul's appeal for a growth in holiness)

10. God is the source of our life in Christ

He is the source of your life in Christ Jesus, whom God made our wisdom, our righteousness and sanctification and redemption...

(I Corinthians 1:30)

This comment of Paul's comes at the end of a discussion on the wisdom of men and the folly of God. The crucifixion of Christ appears to be folly in the view of the worldly wise, but God's apparent folly is far superior to the so called wisdom of men. God chose the weak and seemingly foolish to change the world. His way of changing the whole landscape of human consciousness is to bring us face to face with the crucified and risen Christ. Through the risen Christ he brings us to eternal life, but he also brought us to life in the first place through the Word who was with God at the beginning (see John 1:1).

There is also an immediate sense in which God brings us new life in Christ. God changes us here and now if we accept his invitation to follow Christ in faith. The life in God's kingdom begins where you are at this moment. It is not simply a case of saying, "Today is the first day of the rest of my life." It is more accurately a case of saying, "This is the first day of the rest of my eternal life."

The new life that we inherit from Christ here and now gives us spiritual know how (wisdom), a clearer moral awareness (righteousness), the capacity to grow closer to God (sanctification) and the ability to exchange our old lamps for new (redemption). The traditional words used in translation of Paul's text (the words in brackets) are necessary words, but each generation of Christians needs to unpack them into contemporary language. When the words are unpacked they can then be repacked and used with more understanding.

What does it mean in everyday terms to say that we have a life in Christ Jesus? It means that each morning when we awake that we are aware that he is with us. It means that when we place our heads on the pillow when we go to bed at night that he is with us and will watch over us. It means that whatever we do during each day, however mundane it may appear, he will share it with us. However, it also means that we are his agents in the world, that whatever we do is for him, that every time we do a loving deed, it is for him. Conversely, every time we hurt somebody, we hurt him. Every time we neglect somebody we neglect him.

As our Lord himself said:

"'Lord, when did we see thee hungry and feed thee, or thirsty and give thee drink? And when did we see thee a stranger and welcome thee, or naked and clothe thee? And when did we see thee sick or in prison and visit thee?' And the king will answer them, 'Truly, I say to you, as you did it to one of the least of these my brethren, you did it to me'" (Matthew 25:37-40).

All our joys and all our sorrows, all our successes and all our failures are shared with him. To pray is to seek him at our deepest level perhaps, but to feel and to live each moment through each day is also to be at one with him, provided we let down the barriers that keep him from entering our every thought and action. St John makes this abundantly clear when he quotes Jesus as saying:

"I am praying for them; I am not praying for the world but for those whom thou hast given me, for they are thine, and thine are mine, and I am glorified in them."
(John 17:9-10)

The true way through life is to follow Christ and it is he who bears the light before us on the pilgrim path. To be a Christian is never to be alone, for Christ walks with all who pray in his name. To live the Christian life is to live in Christ. He is the source of all life and in his risen life we are made new each day.

Bible readings

– Philippians 2:14-18 (Holding fast the word of life)
– Colossians 3:1-4 (Your life is hid with Christ in God)

11. God's love is shown in Christ's sacrifice

But God shows his love for us in that while we were yet sinners Christ died for us. Since, therefore, we are now justified by his blood, much more shall we saved by him from the wrath of God.

(Romans 5:8-9)

There seems to be a strange contradiction in this text. God loves us so much that he allowed Christ to die for us to save us from God's wrath. The question that springs to mind is, if God loves us why is he wrathful? To understand God's wrath it is needful to understand that this is not the same as a human emotion, though it is a quality of God in the divine character. God is not given to fits of anger as we are, though of course the incarnate Christ occasionally showed righteous anger (see Mark 11:15-19).

God's wrath is an essential and permanent component of his holiness. When faced with sin or wickedness God's wrath comes into action. Although this is inevitable, it must be remembered that God is not an abstract, but that he has personality. God's love is personal and his wrath is equally personal. However, human love and human wrath are not the same as the divine qualities, though we do use the same words. It must be remembered, as Isaiah wrote:

"For as the heavens are higher than the earth,
so are my ways higher than your ways
and my thoughts than your thoughts" (Isaiah 55:9).

In any case, Paul makes it clear that the sacrifice of Christ is the means by which humans are able to stand in the day of judgement. Repentant sinners are "justified by his blood". (The Greek word for "justify" means "to be made righteous".) This is another piece of traditional theological language that needs teasing out in every day terms, remembering of course that human parallels are always inadequate. But suppose a human parent finds that his (her) six year old child has pulled out most of the beautiful flowers in a neighbour's garden. The parent is wrathful but realises that the child has not fully understood the damage done. However, the child has some appreciation of the hurt caused and says he is sorry both to his parent and to the neighbour. The parent takes the burden of the child's guilt and offers to pay to restock the neighbour's garden. Everyone is reconciled by the parent's action and the child has taken another step in moral growth.

In a similar way, when we have done something wrong, God himself will step in when we express sorrow for our sin. God will accept the responsibility and the punishment for our shortcomings. We, however, have to attempt to put right the wrong we have done to the best of our ability. In the judgmental situation God shows mercy and love, but has to satisfy the demands of justice. So it is that the Father has made the self sacrifice through his Son. It is important to remember though that God is both Father and Son.

As we know, God's self sacrifice involved the shedding of Christ's blood. This has symbolic reference to the old sacrificial system of the temple. Through certain sacrifices the sinner believed he could make atonement for his sin (see Leviticus 4:1-3). But as well as fulfilling and recasting the Old Testament sacrificial system, the sacrifice of Christ looked forward to the new communion of Christ's body and blood in the Eucharist. This was God's own action, not the action of any human being, apart from our Lord, of course.

Paul uses the language of "saving" or salvation. The Greek words used to mean "save" can refer to saving someone from danger or to healing someone. By and large, however, Paul uses the word to refer to spiritual saving. But what does that mean? What does it mean to go through a process of salvation? Sometimes Paul speaks of salvation in the present tense, when he seems to mean that God's grace is with us (cf. I Corinthians 1:18). At other times his use of the word has a future perspective as when he talks about salvation as in the future (cf. Romans 13:11). At other times Paul speaks as if we had already been saved (cf. Romans 8:24). Surely, two conclusions at least may be drawn from this usage. Firstly, salvation is not completed in this life. Secondly, it is a continuing process of growth and change.

Of course, quite often we Christians talk about being saved from our sins. However, when we have been forgiven, we inevitably sin again because of our human weakness. Then yet again we are forgiven, hopefully learning a little more each time and growing towards Christ a little more each time. Perhaps then salvation is a piece of shorthand which describes our spiritual growth. Each of us may be growing towards a kind of perfect blueprint which God has in mind for us, but each soul's final design may well be unique.

Perhaps the Anglican Book of Common prayer captures something of this thought in its translation of the 23rd Psalm:

"He shall convert my soul:
and bring me forth in the paths of righteousness,
for his name's sake" (Psalm 23:3).

Bible readings

– I Timothy 1:12-17 (Christ Jesus came into the world to save sinners)
– Romans 3:21-26 (Justified by God's grace)

NOTE: For *God as Judge* see Chapter XI.

III

Love is all important

1. May your love abound

And it is my prayer that your love may abound more and more, with knowledge and all discernment, so that you may approve what is excellent, and may be pure and blameless for the day of Christ, filled with the fruits of righteousness which come through Jesus Christ, to the glory and praise of God.

(Philippians 1:9-11)

The idea that love should abound is a joyful one and, like laughter, love is infectious. If the whole world abounded with love, what a wonderful world it would be! St Paul certainly did his share of bringing love to the world, but the gift he brought was in the context of his own self discipline and commitment – which were absolute. At the same time, the person who wrote these words must have been filled with a deep sense of God's love and must also have been overflowing with love himself. To have known Paul as closely as Luke did, for example, must have been a heart warming experience.

The word for "love" which Paul usually uses is the Greek word *agapē* and in all the quotations in this chapter this is the word used. Some scholars believe that *agapē* is the sort of love which is based, not on instinctive natural affection, but rather on esteem for someone. To put this in another way, when the will commands love for someone, that is *agapē*. Through this kind of love a person may love someone he has taken a dislike to. However, it is clear from the quotation under discussion that Paul is using *agapē* with a sense of warmth and affection. Otherwise, *agapē* would be as cold as charity, and that does not describe Paul's love. *Agapē*, indeed, may be joined to other kinds of love. For example, if the deeply personal love of marriage should be harnessed to *agapē*, then many marriages would be much more stable, because *agapē* is the sort of love that persists through all the ups and downs of life. In other words, to bring true Christian love to a marriage means a large measure of self giving as well as overt affection.

At the same time, Paul advises that love should be associated with "knowledge and discernment". Perhaps "wisdom" is the most appropriate English word to describe the addition of these two qualities. This shows there is an important difference between romantic love and *agapē*. Romantic love often elbows wisdom out and sometimes unhappiness results. Wise love takes consequences into account. Of course it is of little use explaining this to Romeo and Juliet! But if a person is wishing to show love in the community it is wise to think out a policy and a cost in terms of commitment.

Paul goes on to say that one consequence of applying knowledge and discernment to love should be the acceptance of standards of excellence. Paul seems to mean moral excellence, since he talks about being "pure and blameless". Christian love, then, should not debase the coinage of good behaviour. The end does not justify the means if evil is involved. For example, if a group of people wish to change the social scene in order to bring more care into the community, it would be acceptable to have peaceful protests against the system, but not violent action which would hurt others. Having said that, it is sometimes the case that people have to choose between the lesser of two evils.

Paul is at pains to say that love bears righteous fruits within ourselves, but only through the power of Christ and to the glory of God. People who are genuinely filled with the fruits of righteousness have a joy and a humility which can be observed in their demeanour. This was true of Moses to a remarkable degree, because when he had been praying his face was so bright that people were afraid to approach him (see Exodus 34:29-35). This "holiness of face" may be observed today in some wonderful people, though not to the extent that they need to cover their faces. Some mystics are recorded by artists as having faces which are lit by love of God and the tradition of the halo ascribed to saints in pictures and stained glass windows may be accounted for by this effect. For example, El Greco's *The Vision of St Francis* gives the face of the saint a strange, almost supernatural glow. Yet again, Titian's *The Presentation of the Virgin in the Temple* shows the splendid radiance surrounding the figure of Our Lady as a girl. Love radiates from some people as light beams from spring sunshine. To be that kind of person requires only one talent, the willingness to give love to God and to other people. The invitation is open to all.

Bible readings

– Galatians 5:22-26 (The fruit of the Spirit is love)
– I Timothy 6:11-16 (Aim for righteousness, godliness, faith and love)

2. Rooted and grounded in love

For this reason I bow my knees before the Father, from whom every family in heaven and on earth is named, that according to the riches of his glory he may grant you to be strengthened with might through his Spirit in the inner man, and that Christ may dwell in your hearts through faith; that you, being rooted and grounded in love, may have power to comprehend with all the saints what is the breadth and length and height and depth, and to know the love of Christ which surpasses knowledge, that you may be filled with all the fullness of God. Now to him who by the power at work within us is able to do far more abundantly than all that we

43

ask or think, to him be glory in the church and in Christ
Jesus to all generations, for ever and ever. Amen.

(Ephesians 3:14-21)

To be rooted and grounded in love is to be committed heart and soul from the depths of our being to obeying our Lord's double commandment, that is to love God and to love our neighbour. This is a very effective image because roots bring life and growth to a plant, and in a similar way love will bring life and growth to the soul. According to Paul this love begins with worship. Paul himself bows to the Father in prayer to ask that the faithful may be strengthened through the Spirit and by the indwelling Christ. We, too, should pray for the fellowship of the Church that love may overflow from all Christians into the world community.

When we are rooted and grounded in love we may have an inkling, along with the saints, of the dimensions of God's love. Paul equates the love of God with total reality by describing it as the key to understanding the breadth and length, and the height and depth of all things. This means that the whole of the universe from end to end and from top to bottom, is embraced in the love of God. Further, through God's love we can explore the dimensions of the spiritual world as far as the point where earth and heaven meet. Indeed, the totality of heaven is also contained within the love of God. All aspects of existence, from the smallest creature ever made to the largest galaxy, from the newest soul in heaven to the whole concourse of saints and angels, can only exist because God wills them into being in his all embracing love. This is why every family in heaven and on earth is named from God the Father. Incidentally, the Greek word for Father is *pater* while the word for family is *patria*, so in the Greek the connection is much more evident.

According to Paul, the love of Christ surpasses all knowledge. This is similar to his statement at the end of his great hymn to love in I Corinthians 13 (see section 7 below). This means that the most important quality in human life is available to everyone. A person doesn't have to go to university to learn love. Even the ability to read the daily newspaper is not a necessary qualification to becoming immersed in God's love. Having said that, of course, it is true that a certain amount of knowledge can make our love more meaningful and effective. However, Paul has made his point. Love is more important than knowledge.

To "be filled with the fullness of God" is a wonderful phrase. This is reminiscent of the overflowing cup in Psalm 23 or of the twelve baskets full of fragments left over after the feeding of the multitude. Indeed, the same word is used to describe the full baskets in Mark 6:43 as is used here by Paul. God's love is like a magnificent fountain which flows unceasingly into the whole of his creation. To be aware of this and to feel the power of that love filling the mind and soul and body, is perhaps what Moses meant when he said:

"Hear, O Israel: The Lord your God is one Lord, and you shall love the Lord your God with all your heart, and with all your soul, and with all your might."

(Deuteronomy 6:4-5)

The continuity of this awareness of God's love through the historical times recorded in the Old and New Testaments and in the history of the Church is remarkable. This is no cosmic con trick. This is the genuine twenty four carat article. It is tangible and real within our experience.

God's love shoots through us from the day we breathe;
his love grows deep within the opening flower;
and his love burgeons in our busy hands,
as we become his love each passing hour.

Bible readings

- Ephesians 2:4-7 (The riches of God's love)
- I Corinthians 2:7-13 (What God has prepared for those who love him)

3. Through love be servants of one another

For you were called to freedom, brethren; only do not use your freedom as an opportunity for the flesh, but through love be servants of one another. For the whole law is fulfilled in one word, "You shall love your neighbour as yourself." But if you bite and devour one another take heed that you are not consumed by one another.

(Galatians 5:13-15)

Paul follows our Lord himself, consciously or unconsciously, in choosing the single commandment, "Love your neighbour as yourself", to summarise the whole of the moral law. This law originally appeared in a long list of Jewish laws in the Book of Leviticus (see Lev 19:18). Jesus, it may be remembered, cast a whole new light upon the law by telling the parable of the Good Samaritan, which shows clearly that anyone in need is our neighbour.

In this letter to the Galatian Church Paul is arguing that people should not be tied down by the traditional Jewish laws, especially the one about circumcision. Christ has brought freedom from the old slavery of the Jewish law, which treated people like children. The law did not give people the freedom of individual responsibility. However, the gift of freedom is not to be misused. Once the love of Christ is accepted as a way of life, believers are not expected to wallow in old sins. Paul draws particular attention to the way the Galatians had been attacking each other very much as political groups do today. He draws attention to the destructive nature of party politics within the Christian congregation.

Paul invites the Galatian people to turn from these follies and to try to live up to the Christian vocation by serving one another. This advice is as good today as it was two thousand years ago. Voluntary service is different from the bondage of slavery. The Christian who chooses to serve his or her neighbour is doing so in the freedom and joy of Christ. Our Lord himself gave his disciples an unforgettable lesson when he washed their feet as a servant (see John 13:5-16).

People who run an Oxfam Shop or who collect for Christian Aid are serving Christ, not in a spectacular way, but nevertheless in a valuable way. Though people like Mother Teresa of Calcutta may be exceptional, the little things achieved by the average person are also important. Mother Teresa, of course, did not seek fame. She became famous because she followed our Lord's example of self sacrificial service to an extraordinary degree. She is equally admired by non-Church people as by Christians.

Paul goes on to say that the Christians of Galatia should walk by the Spirit and not by the flesh (Gal 5:16). To walk by the Spirit is to walk in love and the "fruit of the Spirit is love" (v. 22). There are many ways of trying to understand the Holy Spirit and it is impossible for us to reach a full understanding, because the depths of God are unsearchable. However, it is helpful to see that the Spirit is, in one sense at least, the love of God in action. This means that to love is to exist in the Spirit and to exist in the Spirit is to love. Charles Wesley must have had a similar thought when he wrote:

"O thou who camest from above
The fire celestial to impart,
Kindle a flame of sacred love
On the mean altar of my heart."

The freedom which Paul describes is, indeed, a freedom of the human spirit, dwelling within the divine Spirit. Nothing can take away this freedom to love. It is true that human hands may have the power to restrict our movements, but they cannot entirely restrict our thoughts, and certainly no human force can kill the Spirit's love within us. Human beings do some terrible things to each other. However, despite "man's inhumanity to man" (Robert Burns), the flame of love will survive in the most inhumane conditions. In the prisoner of war and concentration camps of the

Second World War wonderful acts of love were performed, not least by Jewish rabbis and Christian chaplains. Human affairs are but temporary structures unless they are built upon God's love. The love of God will accompany us from this world to the next, but the hatred and wickedness of man will create its own self holocaust, will perish in a hell of its own making. Love is the lamp of God which has the power to illuminate the dark recesses of every soul.

Bible readings

- Galatians 5:22-26 (The fruits of the Spirit)
- Ephesians 5:1-2 (Walk in love)

4. Who shall separate us from the love of Christ?

Who shall separate us from the love of Christ? Shall tribulation, or distress, or persecution, or famine, or nakedness, or peril, or sword? As it is written, "For thy sake we are being killed all the day long; we are regarded as sheep to be slaughtered." No, in all these things we are more than conquerors through him who loved us. For I am sure that neither death, nor life, nor angels, nor principalities, nor things present, nor things to come, nor powers, nor height, nor depth, nor anything else in all creation, will be able to separate us from the love of God in Christ Jesus our Lord.

(Romans 8:35-39)

There are many comforting words in the Bible – and this passage is one of the most helpful in practically any situation. Paul himself had many tribulations (see II Corinthians 11:21-29) so he certainly knew what he was talking about. Paul catalogues a number of situations in which it would be impossible to be separated from the love of Christ. Nothing within the height and depth of the universe, and no being in the realm of heaven even, could succeed in negating Christ's love for us. Paul could simply have said, of course, that God's love is everywhere, but that would have been much less effective. It is wonderful to feel that even to the point of death God's love will be with us and, indeed, that it will be waiting for us beyond death.

Faith in Christ brings many gifts and once we have encountered Christ on the pilgrimage through life, his grace and his love are freely available, as well as his guidance and strength. Events in life may take a person to the depths of despair, but in that despair he may meet Christ on his cross. Behind that cross can be seen the glint of hope in the resurrection. From that point Christ will walk with him and lead him to the top of a mountain where the view of heaven is glorious, even though it is seen only partially through a gap in the mists of time.

If you are in hospital waiting to have a serious operation, or if you have recently lost a loved relative, or if you have been made redundant and cannot find a job, or if one of your children has taken the wrong direction in life, or if your house has been destroyed by earthquake or flood, or if your country is overrun by a foreign army – in any of these or a hundred other situations, the love of Christ is with you. To put it in another way, Christ himself is with you. His is the love that will not let you go. His is the love that awaits you every single morning as you awake. As the hymn says:

"New every morning is the love
Our wakening and uprising prove;
Through sleep and darkness safely brought,
Restored to life and power and thought."

(John Keble)

When Christ gave his cry of dereliction on the cross he was quoting from a Hebrew Psalm:

"My God, my God, why hast thou forsaken me?"

(Psalm 22:1)

However, that psalm ends in a triumphant declaration:

> "...men shall tell of the Lord to the coming generation, and proclaim his deliverance to a people unborn..."
>
> (v. 30)

In a similar way, using a quotation from Psalm 44:22, Paul tells us, our situation may be dire, but through Christ's love "we are more than conquerors". Of course, Paul was writing in a context where martyrdom was a possibility for any Christian, and Paul himself was eventually martyred for his faith. In some parts of the world today, it is equally possible that a Christian may have to give his life for Christ. Christian workers slaughtered in Ruanda in 1994 had to face this supreme test. From St Stephen to Dietrich Bonhoeffer and through to the present day, the Christian calling has always carried the possibility of martyrdom. Fortunately, however, there are many parts of the world where Christians can live without persecution.

The world in which we live contains many other perils as well as many wonderful treasures. However, within the computation of all the possible perils that might beset a person in this life, there is one constant treasure, and that is "the love of God in Christ Jesus our Lord". Wherever we go, whatever we do, no power in heaven or on earth can take that love from us.

The words of Minnie Louise Haskins are often quoted, but they are so beautiful that it is worth quoting them again:

> "And I said to the man who stood at the gate of the year: 'Give me a light that I may tread safely into the unknown.' And he replied, 'Go out into the darkness and put your hand into the hand of God. That shall be to you better than light and safer than a known way.'"
>
> (From *God Knows*)

Bible readings

- Romans 8:12-17 (Fellow heirs with Christ)
- II Timothy 1:3-7 (A spirit of power and love and self control)

5. Let love be genuine

Let love be genuine; hate what is evil, hold fast to what is good; love one another with brotherly affection; outdo one another in showing honour. Never flag in zeal, be aglow with the Spirit, serve the Lord. Rejoice in your hope, be patient in tribulation, be constant in prayer. Contribute to the needs of the saints, practise hospitality.

(Romans 12:9-13)

Paul was always full of zeal and he was certainly genuine through and through. When he persecuted the first followers of Christ he did so with might and main (cf. Acts 9:1-2). When Stephen was stoned Paul was very much part of the executing party (Acts 8:1). He confesses in his letter to Philippi that he was "as to zeal a persecutor of the church" (3:6). But it was this same trait in his character that made him so zealous to carry the Gospel to the whole world. When he wrote to the Romans (as above) he could have been describing his own attitude. He never flagged in zeal. He was always "aglow with the Spirit".

What Paul is advising the Romans is that they should preach and practise an actively social Gospel. In order to do this, love must be at the centre of a Christian's life. The other side of the coin is that evil must be cast aside as something hateful. At the same time what is good must be grasped firmly. Paul knew well enough that there is both good and evil within each individual soul. He was very conscious of this inner conflict (Romans 7:18-20). The existence of any evil within the self cannot sit easily with any pilgrimage to perfection, which is what the Christian is called to undertake. Consequently, evil must not be allowed a comfortable seat in the psyche, or it will undoubtedly grow more powerful. Paul, of course, resolved this conflict by the discovery that Christ will fight evil with us and, if we turn to him, will also forgive us, when we fail miserably to control the dark side of our human nature. God's grace is with us in this struggle.

Brotherly affection, as Paul puts it, is the affection that members of the same family should have for each other. Members of the Church should display this family affection towards one another because they are all sons and daughters of God, brothers and sisters of Christ (cf. Galatians 4:6 and II Corinthians 6:18). In addition to regarding each other as brothers and sisters we ought to show honour to one another. Within the family, affection is usually shown, but sometimes familiarity breeds a mild sort of contempt which falls short of honouring our brothers and sisters. Respecting people, including close relations, should be part of our Christian philosophy. Within our congregations, then, and even across congregations, we should show to each other, love, honour and respect. To speak disparagingly of another or to snub someone, is the opposite of showing respect. Even if we sometimes feel antipathy we should never forget the rules of good manners and we should, of course, try to combat our antipathy. We should bend over backwards to show our love to those for whom we have a feeling of dislike.

Paul then mentions two Christian virtues which are now traditional, namely, patience and constancy. Whatever tribulations befall us, we should be patient and we should never give up praying. More than that, we ought to rejoice whatever our situation, because we have been granted an indescribable gift, that is, hope in the love of Christ. God never fails us because he is constant in his love. He is also patient with us when we fall short of our ideals. Distractions abound and too often we hare off in pursuit of some immediate goal whose ultimate value may be dubious. Charles Wesley expressed this thought very well:

"Still let thy love point out my way:
How wondrous things thy love hath wrought!
Still lead me, lest I go astray;
Direct my work, inspire my thought;
And, if I fall, soon may I hear
Thy voice, and know that love is near."

When we recollect ourselves and turn back to Christ he is always there. However, through experience we learn that persistence in prayer and patience in times of difficulty may save us a lot of heartache.

As well as contributing to the needs of the saints (i.e. faithful church members), Paul advises that we should also practice hospitality. The Greek word for hospitality literally means "the loving of strangers". The same word is used in the First Letter to Timothy where church leaders in particular are advised to be "hospitable". The writer of the Letter to the Hebrews is much quoted as advising us "to show hospitality to strangers, for thereby some have entertained angels unawares..." (Hebrews 13:2). (Traditionally Paul was believed to have written the Letter to the Hebrews, but now this is regarded by many as unlikely.)

All in all, the passage under discussion gives us not only sound advice, but a recipe for a happy life.

Bible readings

– Colossians 1:9-14 (Bearing fruit in every good work)
– II Corinthians 1:3-7 (Patient endurance)

6. Love one another

Owe no one anything, except to love one another; for he who loves his neighbour has fulfilled the law. The commandments, "You shall not commit adultery, You shall not kill, You shall not steal, You shall not covet," and any other

53

commandment, are summed up in this sentence, "You shall
love your neighbour as yourself." Love does no wrong to a
neighbour; therefore love is the fulfilling of the law.

(Romans 13:8-10)

While St Paul lists here four of the moral commands
written by Moses, he also says that these and any other
commandment are summed up in the law of love. Of course,
the Jews used a multiplicity of commandments. For example, there are long lists of laws in the Jewish Bible (i.e.
the Old Testament) at Exodus, chapters 21-23; Leviticus,
chapters 17-27; Deuteronomy, chapters 12-26. Paul and his
Jewish contemporaries would have been trained to try to
keep all of these laws and many others which were addi-
tional to the scriptures. Paul is saying, then, that his legal
training as a Pharisee is partly outdated. However, to be
fair to the tradition of the Pharisees, some of the more
enlightened rabbis, for example, Hillel, also preached that
the single law of love covered the whole of the Jewish law.
(Hillel lived approximately between 50 BC and 25 AD)

At the same time, Paul claims that "love is the fulfilling
of the law". This reflects what our Lord himself said in the
Sermon on the Mount:

"Think not that I have come abolish the law and the
prophets; I have come not to abolish them but to fulfil
them" (Matthew 5:17).

Paul also says that the law was a custodian (schoolmas-
ter) (Galatians 3:24). The Greek word used for "custodian"
is the word from which the English word *pedagogue* is
derived (*paidagogos*). In Paul's view, then, the purpose of
the law was to teach people the right way to behave. In that
respect the law is still valid because it gives moral guidelines. However, in the new dispensation of Christ, it is clear
that love alone can satisfy the full requirements of the law.
If a person is filled with the love of Christ this in itself is
the supreme moral agent. Such a person would not break

the moral law because it would not normally be a loving thing to do. Of course, there are a few exceptions when it might be right to break a rule in order to perform a loving act. It is the spirit of the law that matters, not the letter. For example, it might be right to kill a cruel tyrant in order to save the lives of thousands of innocent prisoners. Or it might be right in a war situation to steal food in order to feed a hundred homeless children.

A puzzling question, though, is why God didn't imprint the law of love on every soul in the course of creation. Wouldn't it have made life much easier? People kill each other, mug each other, rape each other, deceive each other, covet other people's jobs, smear people's characters and commit a host of other unpleasant acts. Why did God create people like us, instead of the pure and good people he might have produced? It is not easy to answer this question. However, it may be that God is, in fact, changing us, as we grow, through all our difficulties, into ultimately good people. Possibly the way he has chosen is the best way to do this. Indeed, if God is the Supreme Wisdom, then his method must be the right one. Perhaps we have to learn not to be bad in order to learn to be good.

Bible readings

- Exodus 20 (The Ten Commandments)
- Luke 10:25-37 (Who is my neighbour?)
- John 13:34-35 (Love one another)

7. The greatest of these is love

Love is patient and kind; love is not jealous or boastful; it is not arrogant or rude. Love does not insist on its own way; it is not irritable or resentful; it does not rejoice at wrong, but rejoices in the right. Love bears all things, believes all things, hopes all things, endures all things. So faith, hope and love abide, these three; but the greatest of these is love.

(I Corinthians 13:4-7, 13)

The great hymn to love in I Corinthians 13 is one of the most influential pieces of writing of the Christian centuries. Within the Bible it may be placed alongside the 23rd Psalm, Isaiah 53 and some of our Lord's parables as a masterpiece of spiritual illumination. Perhaps the last verse of Paul's hymn, quoted above, represents the essence of his thought. In that verse he lists the three most important Christian virtues, as faith, hope and love, and then plumps for love as the greatest virtue of all. He writes of faith and hope elsewhere (cf. Galatians 2:15-21, Romans 4:16-18), but in I Corinthians 13 he concentrates on love.

He refers to love as "a still more excellent way" (I Corinthians 12:31b). The comparison is with the gifts of the Spirit described in Chapter 12. Whatever powers of prophecy we have, however strong our faith may be, however deep our knowledge, however generous our gifts to others – these are all of little value without love. A person could be a great writer or musician, or an Oxbridge professor, or a generous supporter of charities, or he could believe firmly in God – but without love these achievements would not be worth anything.

Paul then goes on to give a detailed definition of what love is and what it is not. On the positive side love is patient, kind, enduring, and can survive whatever comes because it is based on a firm faith and a worthy hope. Love does not include jealousy, boastfulness, arrogance, rudeness, selfishness, irritability, resentfulness or delight at the misfortune of others. It would be interesting to devise a questionnaire based on this analysis of the Christian character. How many would each of us score? Do you actually know someone who fits this description? Does the description fit you? If a WANTED advertisement using Paul's description were placed in the press in order to find Christians would you feel able to apply for the post?

Of course, those who felt able to answer such an advertisement and actually did so would probably be disqualified for boastfulness! Christian love, in fact, does not advertise itself, but works underground to change the world. The Gospel of love is designed to change people. Paul himself was hit metaphorically by an earthquake when he met Christ. The whole direction of his life was changed immediately. Such a revolutionary change of attitude and direction is possible for everyone and if every Christian took Paul's description of love as a model and acted upon it there would be an invasion of the world by the powers of the Kingdom of heaven. Of course, that invasion started long ago with Christ, but his present love works through people. Paul's blueprint is clear. It is a handbook on how to put Christian love into practice.

Bible readings

- II Timothy 2:7-13 (Enduring all things)
- II Corinthians 6:1-10 (Enduring in love)

IV

The Cross of Christ within us

1. The life of Jesus manifested in our bodies

But we have this treasure in earthen vessels, to show that the transcendent power belongs to God and not to us. We are afflicted in every way, but not crushed; perplexed, but not driven to despair; persecuted, but not forsaken; struck down, but not destroyed; always carrying in the body the death of Jesus, so that the life of Jesus may also be manifested in our bodies. For while we live we are always being given up to death for Jesus' sake, so that the life of Jesus may be manifested in our mortal flesh. So death is at work in us, but life in you.

(II Corinthians 4:7-12)

Paul very modestly uses "we" in this passage and not "I", though it is obvious that his own experience is behind his view here. However, he feels it right to include other "ambassadors for Christ" (5:20) in his description of the sacrifices made on behalf of the Christian congregation at Corinth. At the same time, the "we" is an invitation to others to follow the same pattern of service despite afflictions and suffering.

The treasure of the Gospel that Paul and his companions have suffered so much to bring, is carried in "earthen vessels". This obviously refers to the human body, but may also refer to the weakness of the flesh in its capacity to sin. The true glory belongs to God and not to man. The "light in our hearts" (v. 6) is given through Christ and no one else apart from Christ can claim the glory due to God.

All the sufferings that Paul has endured are compared to

59

an inner death. Persecution and affliction may come, but these are accepted as a sign of dying for Christ so that new life may grow. This is reminiscent of the parable of the sower (Mark 4:1-20). The seed of Christ, the word of God, grows strongly in the right kind of soil. Those who accept Christ will experience death leading to life within themselves. At the same time the seeds will transfer to others that life may grow in them. This is Paul's point. He and his companions are "always being given up to death for Jesus' sake" and new life grows in them; but new life also grows in those to whom they preach the word of life.

"To carry in the body the death of Jesus" is a very telling phrase. This is making the crucifixion very personal. It is virtually a form of existentialism in the sense that Christ exists in us in a very real way. However, Christ also exists over and beyond ourselves, so this "existentialism" is only a means of describing the close nature of our relationship with him. In any case, the crucifixion within us becomes the resurrection within us and we are transformed. This is the new creation, the second stage of creation that Paul talks about elsewhere (cf. Ephesians 2:10).

In Paul's own case the first stage of his inner transformation was very sudden (cf. Acts 9) but he then had some years to grow spiritually before and during the most important part of his missionary work throughout the Mediterranean world. Paul's life in the years immediately following his conversion are only sketchily dealt with (see Acts 9:30 and cf. Galatians 1:15-2:1). Each individual's spiritual development will vary according to the circumstances and to the starting base. One person may have a sudden conversion, first accepting the cross and resurrection into his personal life, and will then grow to comparative spiritual maturity very quickly. Another may change very slowly without the kind of inward revolution that Paul had. Some may have several changes of mind before finally accepting Christ for life. However, in all of these examples and, indeed, within a range of variations, the power of the "cross within" to change people is indisputable. This power goes right across all shades of tradition in the Church. Ignatius Loyola and St Francis are two examples of people who underwent a radical change of perspective. John Wesley and St Augustine of Hippo each had special experiences which changed their lives. Mary Magdalene is regarded in tradition as the penitent sinner who was transformed to saint by the power of the cross. There are literally millions of ordinary people who have knelt before the cross of Christ and have accepted its power to change. It does not take a prophet to foretell that this kind of experience will continue to happen to people in future centuries.

Bible readings

– Acts 13:16-33 (Paul preaches the Gospel)
– John 19 (John recalls the crucifixion)

2. The folly of the cross

For the word of the cross is folly to those who are perishing, but to those who are being saved it is the power of God. For it is written,
  "I will destroy the wisdom of the wise,
  and the cleverness of the clever I will thwart."

(I Corinthians 1:18-19)

Although Paul is writing to a particular situation, his words are universally true. The idea of God's Son being executed by crucifixion seems to be preposterous. However, the subsequent resurrection and our later understanding of Christ's work on the cross show God's "folly" to be wisdom almost beyond human understanding.

The specific situation in Corinth which Paul is addressing is the problem of factional loyalties. Some of the congregation are expressing loyalty to Paul, others to Apollos, yet others to Cephas (Peter) and some to Christ. Paul exposes such divisions as destructive to the Christian fellowship. The "word of the cross" puts human pretensions in their place.

Cephas (Peter) is better known than Apollos but it is not certain that Cephas ever went to Corinth. Apollos, however, certainly did, because he is the one Paul mentions as watering the plants put in by Paul himself (see 3:5-9). It may or may not be significant that the Greek word for "I will destroy" in verse 19 is *apolo*. In that verse Paul is referring to Isaiah 29:14 and the text in the Greek version of the Old Testament begins with this word, as does Paul's loose quotation. Even if Paul is being sarcastic with a deliberate pun, he later pours oil on troubled waters by saying that he and Apollos are "God's fellow workers" (3:9).

In referring to God's wisdom Paul was certainly aware of the Jewish tradition about the divine wisdom in the Book of Proverbs and elsewhere. In the Book of Proverbs the writer claims that God created Wisdom before he made the universe (8:22). The writer also implies that Wisdom was beside God at creation "like a master workman" (Proverbs 8:30), though the text is uncertain at that point. Some people go on to argue that it was Christ who was the divine Wisdom, much as John claims he was the divine Word at the beginning of creation (John 1:1). This makes Paul's comment about human wisdom even more pointed.

Paul goes on to say that not only does the cross seem foolish to supposedly wise Gentiles (possibly Greek philosophers and Gnostics), but that it is a "stumbling block to Jews" (v. 23). This is probably a reference to Jewish law which states that a man hanged on a tree "is accursed by God" (Deuteronomy 21:23). Paul discusses the same idea at Galatians 3:13. To Jewish legalists, then, the death of God's true Messiah by crucifixion would be inconceivable. Consequently, many Jews found the cross of Christ a stumbling block.

To many people today the word of the cross still seems to be foolish. If a person's main aim in life is to make money, or to gain power, or to become famous, then indeed, the cross must seem foolish. But the poet Thomas Gray in his famous *Elegy in a Country Church-yard* wrote:

"...And all that beauty, all that wealth e'er gave,
Awaits alike th'inevitable hour,
The paths of glory lead but to the grave."

This may be a sombre viewpoint, but it is the truth. In the same way, the cross leads to the truth in each one of us. If we live with the cross we live with Christ, both in his humility and in his glory. Christ's path of glory led beyond the grave. This does not mean we have to live a joyless life with no thought but death. On the contrary, God expects us to lead a full and joyful life and to use the wonderful gifts he has given to us. Our Lord himself enjoyed looking at the spring flowers (Matthew 6:28-29) or going to parties (John 2:1-11). However, he was more aware than we are that our true destiny lies beyond the cross into the new and glorious life of the resurrection.

Bible readings

– I Corinthians 3:18-23 (Become a fool to become wise)
– Ephesians 1:15-23 (The spirit of wisdom)

3. Christ our paschal lamb

For Christ, our paschal lamb, has been sacrificed. Let us, therefore, celebrate the festival, not with the old leaven, the leaven of malice and evil, but with unleavened bread of sincerity and truth.

(I Corinthians 5:7b-8)

There is a considerable amount of deep theological think-ing concentrated in these two sentences, including a radical reinterpretation of the Jewish faith. The paschal lamb was (and still is) eaten at the feast of the Passover to remind each Jewish family of the Exodus. It was through the Exodus that God redeemed his people from slavery (see Exodus 12). Of course, Christians accept that the Exodus was a mighty act of God on behalf of his chosen people, but the point of Paul's new thinking is that God has per-formed an even mightier act of redemption through Christ's "Passover" sacrifice.

The occasion which gives rise to Paul's comments is the sin of a member of the congregation who is living with his father's wife, presumably meaning his step-mother (v. 1). This was against Roman law and also against Jewish law (cf. Leviticus 18:7ff.). Paul is scandalised and demands the removal of the man from the fellowship. This is for the man's own ultimate good. Then Paul goes on to use the comparison with leaven (yeast), meaning that evil can spread throughout a whole community if not dealt with at its outset. Not many people bake their own bread nowadays, but those who do, know that a small amount of yeast has a transforming effect on the whole of the dough. In the comparison Paul points out that if the leaven is evil, then the whole lump of dough will be evil. If, however, the leaven is good, then the whole lump will become good.

The point about Christ being the paschal (Passover) lamb, almost incidentally referred to here by Paul, is that the whole of the Jewish sacrificial system has been re-placed by the sacrifice of Christ. At the same time, this new sacrifice has the effect of redeeming the whole of human-kind from sin. In other words, Paul is expressing the deep inner meaning of Christianity in a couple of sentences as part of an ethical argument. Strangely, Paul does not else-where expand this idea of Christ as the paschal lamb, though it obviously lies deep within his thinking and lies behind such passages as Ephesians 1:3-14, Colossians 1:13-14 and some of the other passages discussed in this chapter.

The mention of unleavened bread gives another dimension to the discussion. Before the Passover, Jewish people search their houses to make sure there is no leaven (yeast) left in the house. During the festival only unleavened bread is eaten. Such bread is perhaps less palatable than leavened bread, but of course its use is symbolic of the haste in which the Jews left Egypt in the Exodus. There wasn't time to allow the dough to rise. In Christian tradition unleavened bread has usually been eaten at the Eucharist, though some groups use ordinary bread and the use of the latter is becoming more common. Paul, of course, is aware of the implicit reference to the Eucharist in his mention of bread and he charges the congregation to associate the eating of the unleavened bread with "sincerity and truth" and to put aside the old leaven of "malice and evil".

It is clear that Paul's advice stands for church congregations today. While it is true that Paul would insist upon a real emphasis on Christian love and forgiveness, nevertheless there should be a limit to our definition of acceptable behaviour. Some people prefer to condemn the sin but to try to love the sinner. This is a good principle, but even that philosophy may have its limits. Certain actions cannot be tolerated within the congregation until repentance and restitution are complete. The treasurer who fiddles the funds may be forgiven after a time, depending on the circumstances, but vicious bullying, pimping or drug trafficking may need more time to eradicate. Does this mean that the serial killer, for example, can never be forgiven? Perhaps we may never know the answer to that question, because we never know the full circumstances. Ultimately only God has the power to forgive.

The difficulty in our day to day running of the Church is to obtain the right balance between tolerance and love on the one hand, and standards of righteousness and judgement on the other hand. Certainly our Lord said, "Judge not, that you be not judged" (Matthew 7:1), but he also said, "Every tree that does not bear good fruit is cut down and thrown into the fire" (Matthew 7:19). Sometimes the action we should take is clear, as it was for St Paul on this occasion. At other times we may have to pray to the Holy Spirit for guidance.

Bible readings

- Romans 12:14-21 (Do not be overcome by evil)
- II Corinthians 1:12-14 (Holiness and godly sincerity)

4. In him we have redemption

In him we have redemption through his blood, the forgiveness of our trespasses, according to the riches of his grace which he lavished upon us.

(Ephesians 1:7)

For there is no distinction; since all have sinned and fall short of the glory of God, they are justified by his grace as a gift, through the redemption which is in Christ Jesus, whom God put forward as an expiation by his blood, to be received by faith.

(Romans 3: 22b-25a)

"Lifeblood" is an important word in our vocabulary. We also have a horror of "bloodshed". Yet Christ's lifeblood was shed at the human level, to become the blood of life at the spiritual level. This is especially significant in the Eucharist. However, this train of thought needs a little explanation.

The idea of "redemption through his blood" must be a very odd one to a person who comes to it without any knowledge of the background. The story of the redemption of the Jewish slaves from Egypt has been referred to in the previous section (and see Exodus 12). In modern terminology redemption is more associated with the pawnbroker or with petrol tokens than with religion. To redeem something today means to exchange money or tokens to obtain something of value or to recover something that has been pawned. Yet the word may still be used in connection with setting someone free for a ransom. This is perhaps the most helpful meaning in trying to understand the biblical concept. Christ "sets us free" or "redeems" us through his blood.

The idea still bristles with possible misunderstandings, even when the meaning of the word "redeem" has been clarified. Other words are used apparently with a similar meaning to redemption, for example, "expiation" and "justification". This adds to the confusion and longish words can be a little off putting. However, "expiate" simply means "to pay the penalty" for something – an idea familiar on the football ground. (The Greek word may also mean "mercy seat".) "Justify" means "to make a person right". All of these rather technical words are really about God forgiving our sins. Christ redeems (frees) us from sin; he pays the penalty for our sin; he makes us right again after we have sinned. Each of these three processes is slightly different, but they add up to make a wonderful gift from God, a special showing of his grace.

In the above passage from Romans (3:22b-25a), Paul maintains that all human beings have sinned. Earlier in the same chapter he gives a patchwork of quotations and references from several psalms and from the Book of Isaiah to make this point very strongly (vv. 10-18). This judgement applies both to Jews and to Gentiles. The law shows that no human being is perfect and that all are accountable to God (3:19). Paul then goes on to say that the law cannot be of any help in saving us from the consequences of our sins. However, redemption (freedom) from our sins may be received through faith in Christ because he leads us to the mercy seat (see Exodus 37:6 and Hebrews 9:5) where God's forgiveness is received.

If a person today feels guilty because he or she has done something wrong, how is it possible to relate to God and to receive his forgiveness? It must first be said that only God has the power to forgive sins and in the case of Christianity the definition of God includes the Father and the Son and the Holy Spirit. Telling God about our sins may be done in different ways. First of all this may be done in private prayer. Secondly, it may be done through oral confession to a priest and that too is private. Thirdly, many church services include a form of confession and this is done corporately by everyone present. Fourthly, any of the above forms may be used to approach God in the Eucharist (that is, Holy Communion or the Mass or the Lord's Supper). Sometimes an individual confession in public is used, though rarely nowadays. The same person may use all of these forms at different times. However, in relation to the discussion of redemption through the blood of Christ, it must be said that the Eucharist is a wonderful way to experience forgiveness and renewal through Christ. Often this forgiveness is expressed by a minister or priest to show that God has forgiven all concerned who have genuinely repented (decided to turn over a new leaf).

Bible readings

– Romans 5:6-11 (While we were yet sinners Christ died for us)
– Colossians 1:21-23 (Reconciled in his body)

5. Christ Jesus came into the world to save sinners

The saying is sure and worthy of full acceptance, that Christ Jesus came into the world to save sinners. And I am the foremost of sinners; but I received mercy for this reason, that in me, as the foremost, Jesus Christ might display his perfect patience for an example to those who were to believe in him for eternal life. To the King of ages, immortal, invisible, the only God, be honour and glory for ever and ever. Amen.

(I Timothy 1:15-17)

This passage makes clear that one of the purposes of Christ's Incarnation was to save sinners. Paul, possibly thinking of the time when he persecuted the Church, maintains that he is the foremost of sinners. This genuine humility of Paul's is to be contrasted with the greatness of his achievements. It is obvious to everyone that he was the apostle to the Gentiles par excellence.

The idea of salvation or saving has already been discussed, but it is worth repeating that with most people this is a process of development and growth, a movement from sin to grace, a transformation from indiscipline to holiness. However, Paul makes an interesting point which is often missed. Although Paul feels he was deeply immersed in sin, yet he knows that Christ has been patient with him in the transformation he is still undergoing. Indeed, says Paul, Christ has used me as an example of how patient he can be with those who do hurtful things. The implication of Paul's claim is, and it is greatly to his credit, that if Christ has been so patient with him, Paul, there is hope for others who may be a great trial to our Lord in their attempted relationship with God.

The doxology (a giving of glory to God) in verse 17 is a wonderful prayer. It is interesting that Paul places this prayer here, just after his confession that he is a sinner. This is reminiscent of Isaiah's confession of his unworthiness when he was so conscious of the holiness of God (see Isaiah 6:3-5). Similarly, it is clear that Paul's vision of God is a blinding glimpse of the immortal King of all time and space. This makes him feel even more unworthy. Yet, like Isaiah, he had been specially chosen by God to do a mighty work. It is this view of God which inspires him to greater missionary efforts, to greater prayerfulness. There are powerful forces working in Paul's soul and mind. Not only has the cross brought him new inner life, not only has he been set free (redeemed) from sin, but he has the vision glorious of God on his throne in the heavenly Jerusalem. Our understanding of what made Paul tick, even if only partial, may help us in our inner lives. His vision may become our vision. His transformation may inspire our transformation. The author of the Book of Proverbs was right when he wrote; "Where there is no vision the people perish" (Proverbs 29:18, Authorised Version).

Bible readings

- Romans 11:25-32 (God's mercy)
- Titus 3:3-8 (Justified by his grace)

6. God sent forth his Son to redeem those under the law

So with us; when we were children, we were slaves to the elemental spirits of the universe. But when the time had fully come, God sent forth his Son, born of woman, born under the law, to redeem those who were under the law, so that we might receive adoption as sons.

(Galatians 4:3-5)

Here again Paul proclaims the Gospel of redemption. He also proclaims the Incarnation in terms that confirm the identity of Christ as the Son of God and as the son of Mary. Paul does not say, either here or elsewhere, whether or not he believed that Our Lady had a virginal conception. However, Luke was a great friend and colleague of Paul's and it is from Luke that we receive much of our information about the birth of Jesus. It is reasonable to deduce from this association with Luke that Paul accepted the doctrine of the Virgin Birth. There is no reason why he should give biographical details about Jesus in his letters. What he does, though, is to state the theological principle of the Incarnation very clearly. Jesus was born of woman, and therefore fully a human being. He was the Son of God and therefore he was divine.

It is interesting that Paul sees redemption as a process

70

by which any human being may become an adopted child of God. Paul uses this phrase several times, usually about Christians (see Romans 8:15; Ephesians 1:5) and once about Israel (Romans 9:4). Before Christ's coming people were like young children and in a similar position to slaves. Sometimes, indeed, slaves were adopted as children by their masters and mistresses. Paul uses this terminology several times (see, for example, Romans 8:15). Once slaves were adopted they would have the same rights as natural children. However, most children then were much more subservient to their parents than children of today. Paul's point is that freedom in Christ brings us to maturity. Slaves who had been adopted would be freed when they came of age, in the same way as natural children.

Those who have brought up children will be aware that it is wise to allow freedom and personal responsibility gradually in relation to the stage of maturity reached. Paul is similarly concerned for the spiritual development of the Galatians. He refers to them as little children in whom Christ is not yet fully formed (Galatians 4:19). He then uses the first born sons of Hagar and Sarah respectively as a comparison (vv. 21-31). Ishmael was the child of the female slave, Hagar, but Isaac was the child of the free woman, Sarah. The child of the slave was cast out and he represents the old covenant; but the child of the free woman represents the new covenant, Paul insists that the members of the Galatian church must regard themselves as children of freedom. In other words, they have to come to something approaching spiritual maturity. They are not behaving as they ought to (5:13). They must learn to live and walk by the Spirit (5:25-26).

This advice is for all of us. Redemption is a process of spiritual change. It is a change of outlook. It is a change of behaviour. It is a development of potential. This process is internal as well as external. Our patterns of thinking need to conform to Christ and to his commandment of love (see Galatians 5:14).

It is a very significant change of emphasis for Paul to

say that the Galatians should "through love be servants of one another" (5:13). This is the use to which their freedom and maturity should be put. They are not to be slaves in the compulsory sense. Like Christ, they ought to be voluntary servants to others. In fact the Greek word for slave is the same as the word for servant; so instead of "being *slaves* to the elementary spirits of the universe" (possibly demonic powers) (see 4:3 above) we should be *slaves* of one another (5:13). One of the difficulties of Biblical language for us is the cultural difference between our world and the world of the Bible. The word "slave" has bad associations for us whereas slavery was accepted as part of normal life in the Roman world. Nevertheless the point is clear, and if we needed any confirmation we would only have to read once again the story about Jesus washing the disciples' feet (John 13:2-20). It would be wonderful, indeed, for each of us to be met by our Lord at the gates of heaven and for him to say, "Well done, good servant!" (Luke 19:17).

Bible readings

– Romans 7:4-6 (The new life of the Spirit)
– Romans 8:12-17 (The spirit of sonship)

7. One mediator between God and man

For there is one God, and there is one mediator between God and men, the man Christ Jesus, who gave himself as a ransom for all, the testimony to which was borne at the proper time. For this I was appointed a preacher and apostle (I am telling the truth, I am not lying), a teacher of the Gentiles in faith and truth.

(I Timothy 2:5-7)

The word "mediator" is used widely today to refer to somebody who acts as a go-between in a dispute between two parties. In the case of Jesus it is not so much a dispute that is involved. It is more a case of a gap that needs to be bridged. God is a unique and all powerful being, whereas human beings are wearing L plates in their journey towards a deeper understanding of God and his purposes in creating the universe. To put this in slightly more technical language, God is perfectly loving and holier than we can ever imagine. We, on the other hand, are growing towards him in love and holiness, but we need some driving lessons to help us in our pilgrimage. The incarnation of God's Son provided the right kind of guidance, a map for the road ahead, if you like.

Of course, the mediation that Christ undertook and still pursues is also about reconciling differences, though not in the sort of argument employers might have with a trade union. God's moral character is such that our imperfections are "uncomfortable" for him to bear. However, he has made us that way: he has placed within us the possibility of doing what is right or of doing what is wrong. So that we can draw closer to him, despite our imperfections, God has given us a mediator who is both one of us and also one with the Godhead. This is an amazing strategy on God's part. Through Christ we can be reconciled with God, we can live in his love and we can begin to understand a little of what holiness means. In this position we can start up the motors of self motivation. When we begin to understand the riches of God's love and the nature of the wonderful life ahead, we are able to align our wills with God's will. Because Christ is within us we can be at one with him, and so at one with God. That is what the mediating work of Christ is about.

The idea of ransom has been discussed above in relation to "redemption". We use the word "ransom" today mostly in connection with kidnapping. This may be a useful parallel. It could be said that we are captured by our own desires and instincts. In order to set us free a ransom needs to be paid. Christ has paid the ransom price and so we are freed, if not from our basic desires at least from their consequences in terms of judgement. But it is still true that if we are living close to Christ we can channel our basic desires into positive and creative channels, and can become aware of our growing freedom to act with love.

Paul feels very strongly that he has been called to witness to this wonderful act of God. He describes himself as both a preacher and an apostle. The word "apostle" means messenger and in the biblical context it usually means God's messenger. To be a preacher is to announce the gospel in a particular way. In the Church this usually means to stand up in front of a congregation and to speak to people about some aspect of God's revelation. However, it is possible to be an apostle in other ways. You may not feel called to stand in a pulpit, but you can still be an apostle and you can still bring the good news of Christ the mediator to other people. One simple way to do this is to remain faithful to your vocation as a Christian. Going to church regularly is a way of witnessing. Helping other people in the name of Christ is another way of giving testimony. What we are called to do is to use our freedom in Christ to use whatever gifts we have been given in his service. As Charles Wesley wrote in a famous hymn:

"Forth in thy name, O Lord, I go,
My daily labour to pursue;
Thee, only thee, resolved to know,
In all I think or speak or do."

Bible readings

– Matthew 20:20-28 (To give his life as a ransom for many)
– Acts 22:12-16 (A witness to all men)

8. The world has been crucified to me

But far be it from me to glory except in the cross of our Lord Jesus Christ, by which the world has been crucified to me, and I to the world.

(Galatians 6:14)

This profound statement is dropped almost casually in a final comment, at the close of the letter, in Paul's "own hand". He would have been dictating to a scribe, but wished to end the letter in a more personal way. For some reason he wrote in large letters (v. 11). Possibly this was to emphasise his personal authorship of the letter or to emphasise his reaction to a particular point of dispute among the congregation. There had obviously been open division about the question of circumcision.

In contrast to this desire of some people to glory "in the flesh", Paul argues that the only worthwhile cause for glory is the cross of Christ. The cross was normally a symbol of shame and degradation, but Paul claims that the cross is actually God's way of changing the world both corporately and individually. It is a new creation that is involved (v. 15). The whole of humankind will be changed by the cross, and at the same time the internal life of each Christian may be changed.

Sometimes the striking originality of some biblical statements goes unnoticed because their content has become part of our Christian culture. To claim that "the world has been crucified to me, and I to the world" is an astonishing statement. It is true that Jesus himself indicated that the cross was to become an individual spiritual force when he said, "If any man would come after me, let him deny himself and take up his cross and follow me" (Mark 8:34). But Paul, above all other biblical writers, internalises the cross and thus fulfils the words and actions of Jesus at the individual spiritual level.

It is true, of course, that Christians have to live in the world and if they wish to change it they may have to be close to it. However, the "world" in Paul's statement refers to the unenlightened standards by which many of us live much of our lives. To be a true follower of Christ we ought to reject such standards even if we have to live alongside them. The cross upon which Christ was hung in almost unimaginable pain is in itself a power which will help us to crucify our worst selves. To live close to Christ in this world is to be part of his incarnational experience. The whole Church is Christ's body in one sense and each individual is a cell within that body. However, the crucified Christ is the risen Christ and the result of crucifying ourselves to the world is not deprivation but rather the embracing of a new and glorious world, the new creation of the risen Christ.

In verse 17 Paul claims that he bears on his body the marks of Jesus. There is no evidence that Paul bore the stigmata as such in the way that St Francis did. More probably he is referring to the physical scars of his beatings and other trials he had undergone in the name of Christ. In Paul's case, and indeed in the case of many other Christians, the call to follow Christ has involved physical torture as well as spiritual discipline. Even so, Paul finds that the cross is a matter for joy and glory because it has the capacity to bring the believer close to Christ.

Of course, it is all very well to theorise about crucifying the self with Christ, but how does that match up with the newspapers we read every day or the television programmes we watch with monotonous regularity? Again, how do we react in social contacts at work or at the golf club? Fortunately, Paul does give us advice elsewhere:

"I wrote to you in my letter not to associate with immoral men; not at all meaning the immoral of this world, or the greedy and robbers, or idolaters, since then you would need to go out of the world."

(I Corinthians 5:9-10)

It is true that some religious do forsake the world by

entering enclosed orders and some additionally even undertake a regime of silence. However, most of us have to remain in the everyday world, so how do we cope with the seamy side of human life when there is no escaping its presence? Perhaps the answer is to be untouched by it. "To the pure all things are pure" (Titus 1:15), and if we are living in the fellowship of Christ we are able to work to change the world without conforming to its lowest standards. To do this we must rely upon God's grace.

Bible readings

– Titus 2:11-15 (Renounce irreligion and worldly passions)
– Ephesians 2:1-7 (Alive together with Christ)

9. Reconciliation through the cross

But now in Christ Jesus you who once were far off have been brought near in the blood of Christ. For he is our peace, who has made us both one, and has broken down the dividing wall of hostility, by abolishing in his flesh the law of commandments and ordinances, that he might create in himself one new man in place of the two, so making peace, and might reconcile us both to God in one body through the cross, thereby bringing the hostility to an end.

(Ephesians 2:13-16)

This passage illustrates yet another dimension of the work of Christ in his sacrifice of himself upon the cross. Before the time of Christ the Jewish nation had tried to separate itself from all other nations. Indeed, they had regarded themselves as God's chosen people, set apart for a special vocation. The Gentiles did not belong to the people of God and were certainly regarded as aliens who were potential enemies of both God and his people.

The reconciliation brought about by Christ is not only between God and sinful humanity, but also between groups of people separated from each other. Paul actually sees this reconciliation as one between Jews and other races, but of course, it is also applicable to any situation where nations or groups are at enmity with each other. If people truly turn to Christ any enmity will be healed and peace will reign. The way Paul expresses this provides another example of his wonderful insight into God's purposes. Christ has created in himself "one new man in place of the two". In other words, all human beings are potentially at one with Christ and with each other.

Of course, it is all very well to talk about reconciliation, but when we are face to face with the opposition it is not easy to make progress. If we hate the sight of somebody, for whatever reason, it is not easy to replace the dislike with love and peace. Furthermore, somebody has to make the first move. It is to be hoped, in any situation of conflict, that if Christians are present they would be prepared to bring the spirit of Christ's love forward.

The word "peace" would have several dimensions for Paul, though to be sure he has in mind the end of hostilities between Jews and Gentiles. But to a Jew, "peace" (Hebrew *shalôm*, Greek *eirēnē* involved prosperity and well being, as well as the end of war. Christ brings peace in its fullness to all who turn to him, so the Christ created human being, whatever his or her race, has access to a deep well of peace which is the love of Christ within. When groups of people really live Christ's peace with each other and within themselves, their lives together should have the richness and vitality of the Kingdom of heaven. Every church congregation is or should be a colony of heaven and a powerhouse of love.

In verse 19, just following the passage under discussion, Paul emphasises his message of reconciliation by showing that the members of the Church "are fellow citizens with the saints and members of the household of God..." People who belong to one nation are fellow citizens and people who are within a single family are members of the same household. These metaphors express very clearly the sort of community that Christians belong to. Unhappily, this quality of fellowship is not always clearly visible to those outside the Church.

Paul goes on to say (vv. 20-22) that Christ is the corner stone of the temple of which all Christians are a part. Yet, this temple is a growing organism, not entirely like a building. In other words the true Church is made of people, not of bricks and mortar. The whole structure of the living Church is God's temple. At the same time each person within this growing Church is a temple for the Holy Spirit.

Paul's concept of the Church is many faceted. He uses vivid metaphors and, indeed, sometimes mixes them, but always in an effective way. The common factor in all his descriptions of the Church and its fellowship is that the crucified and risen Christ is, in effect, the heart and head of the Church and of God's Kingdom upon earth. The first verse of a hymn by S.J. Stone expresses this very well:

"The Church's one foundation
Is Jesus Christ her Lord;
She is his new creation
By water and the word:
From heaven he came and sought her
To be his holy bride;
With his own blood he bought her
And for her life he died."

Bible readings

– II Corinthians 5:20-21 (Be reconciled to God)
– Colossians 1:15-20 (Making peace by the blood of his cross)

V

Risen with Christ

1. Raised on the third day

*For I delivered to you as of first importance what I also
received, that Christ died for our sins in accordance with
the scriptures, that he was buried, that he was raised on the
third day in accordance with the scriptures, and that he
appeared to Cephas, then to the twelve. Then he appeared
to more than five hundred brethren at one time, most of
whom are still alive, though some have fallen asleep. Then
he appeared to James, then to all the apostles. Last of all,
as to one untimely born, he appeared also to me.*

(I Corinthians 15:3-8)

This part of Paul's first letter to the Corinthian Church
sounds like a set formula or part of a creed, possibly used in
worship. Paul is proclaiming the known facts of Christ's
resurrection and lists the key witnesses who had seen the
risen Christ. This basic information had been passed to
Paul by other members of the Church and he in turn had
previously passed it on to the Corinthians. He is now reminding them of that same essential core of the Christian
faith, presumably because questions were being raised by
members of the congregation.

Peter (Cephas) is named as a primary witness and not
just as one of the twelve (cf. Luke 24:34). Some manuscripts say "eleven" rather than "twelve", but of course
Judas Iscariot's replacement (Matthias) would certainly
have been a witness to the resurrection anyway. James, the
Lord's brother, is also mentioned by name. He was a leading member of the Church in Jerusalem (Galatians 1:19).

Paul's information does not match the Gospel accounts precisely, but then the Gospels do not agree with one another in every detail. (E.g. Who precisely went to the tomb first? Was there one angel or were there two at the tomb?) It is likely that Paul's account is the first written statement available to us, though it is obviously not in narrative form as the Gospels are. The first oral accounts must have come from the actual witnesses, many of whom were still alive when Paul was writing his letter to Corinth. The account produced by Paul is a summary of the original first hand resurrection stories.

Paul includes himself among the witnesses to the appearances of Christ after the resurrection. There are three accounts of his conversion experience in Acts of the Apostles and these indicate that Paul's experience was auditory rather than visual, apart from the light which blinded him (Acts 9:1-19; 22:3-11; 26:12-18). Of course, the experience of Paul was an authentic resurrection "appearance" because the person who spoke to Paul identified himself as Jesus. Paul's conviction that he had met the risen Christ accounts for his dedication of the rest of his life to proclaiming the Gospel. What else could have changed him so radically and permanently? At the same time, he modestly says that he is unfit to be called an apostle because of his earlier persecution of the Church, but he continues, "...by the grace of God I am what I am..." (v. 10).

It is interesting that Paul, a trained Pharisee steeped in the Jewish scriptures, should claim that Christ died for our sins "according to the scriptures". The New Testament writers searched the Old Testament for proof texts to show that Jesus was the messiah. These texts are often quoted (see for example Romans 9:33, 10:11 and Isaiah 28:16). Jesus himself, of course, saw himself as fulfilling the scriptures. When he met the two men on the road to Emmaus he talked with them: "And beginning with Moses and all the prophets, he interpreted to them in all the scriptures the things concerning himself" (Luke 24:27). The idea that Christ's coming was foretold by earlier generations and that this was all in God's great plan to reveal himself to the world is wonderful indeed.

A genuine seeker for the truth may say, "But that's all very well, the so called resurrection took place a long time ago. But how do we know today that this event truly happened?" It is easy to give a pat answer by suggesting that it is necessary to have faith and all will be revealed. The fact is, the conviction that the resurrection really happened has to be very personal. It is vitally important, because without a belief in the resurrection it is not possible to be a Christian in any real sense, though one may nevertheless accept the teaching of Jesus. Some people argue that Christianity is caught rather than taught. This implies that people who convincingly express their testimony to Christ today may convince others of the truth about Christ. It is surely true that testimony or "witnessing" has always been an important in Christian teaching.

Different people may give differing advice to the seeker. However, many people who have sought Christ in puzzlement have found him in certainty, or to be more accurate, he has found them. As our Lord himself said, "You did not choose me, but I chose you..." (John 15:16). Conviction comes to some through reading the Bible, to others through reading about the great saints, to others through a significant encounter with a believing Christian, to a few perhaps through a supernatural experience in answer to a prayer. One thing is certain, those who have been found by Christ are not in any doubt about his presence with them. To paraphrase a famous saying of Descartes some could undoubtedly say, "Christ is, therefore I am a Christian."

Bible readings

- Mark 8:31-38 (The Son of man must suffer many things)
- Mark 16:1-8 (The empty tomb)

2. The dead will be raised imperishable

Lo! I tell you a mystery. We shall not all sleep, but we shall all be changed, in a moment, in the twinkling of an eye, at the last trumpet. For the trumpet will sound, and the dead will be raised imperishable, and we shall be changed. For this imperishable nature must put on the imperishable, and this mortal nature must put on immortality.

(I Corinthians 15:51-54)

Much of Chapter 15 of Paul's second letter to Corinth is devoted to the nature of the resurrection. He believes that the physical bodies we use in this life will be replaced by spiritual bodies in the resurrection life (see verses 42-44). The verses quoted above are the climax of a wonderful description of the new, imperishable life of heaven. The great difficulty with Paul's thought here is that he seems to be expecting Christ to come again very soon. Given the reality of his own experience on the Damascus road, it is not surprising that he should believe the "parousia" (Second Coming) to be imminent (see v. 22 of I Corinthians 15).

At the coming of Christ both the living and the dead will be instantly transformed. All the faithful will become their immortal selves in their imperishable, resurrection bodies. As Christ has conquered death (v. 54) he has also conquered the power of sin, which Paul almost equates with the law. Of course, he means that breaking the law is sinful. However, because of his reaction against his earlier training as a Pharisee, he obviously feels very strongly that the Jewish law points to sin, whereas Christ points to grace and new life.

To describe the resurrection life Paul uses a series of comparisons with the natural world and with the heavenly bodies (vv. 35-41). He then uses the imagery of the first man and the man of heaven, comparing Adam and Christ: "Just as we have borne the image of the man of dust, we shall also bear the image of the man of heaven" (v. 49).

Perhaps in a more scientific age we can see more clearly the possibility of other dimensions than our own which may provide the parameters of heaven. Is heaven multidimensional, rather than three dimensional? Do the saints and angels have access to powers that we cannot even imagine? Inevitably our ideas of heaven and the nature of the resurrection body are speculative. The only guide we have is the nature of the body of the risen Jesus. During his post resurrection appearances Jesus could distribute fish (John 21:13) and had a body solid enough to be touched (John 20:27). Yet, he could appear as if from nowhere and walk through closed doors (John 20:19). Instead of seeing these accounts as inconsistent, as some people insist upon doing, perhaps we should consider that the risen Son of God, and perhaps also saints and angels, might have powers beyond our scientific knowledge.

Paul was wrong in believing that Christ would come again in his (Paul's) lifetime. That does not necessarily mean that his description of the Second Coming was untrue. In fact some of the writers of the Bible specialised in prophecies about the "end time" and claimed to have special revelations. Daniel and the Book of Revelation are examples of that kind of literature, usually called apocalyptic literature. Daniel for example wrote a description of the Son of man coming in glory to rule the world (Daniel 7:13-14). The Book of Revelation describes the new heaven and the new earth that God will bring about (21:1-4) and at the end of the book is a prophecy of Christ's Second Coming:

"He who testifies to these things says, 'Surely I am coming soon.' Amen. Come, Lord Jesus!"

(Revelation 22:20)

Paul, then, is writing in a well known style when he prophesies that Christ will come again soon. To be fair to Paul he also writes that the exact time of the Day of the Lord is secret:

"For you yourselves know well that the day of the Lord
will come like a thief in the night."

(I Thessalonians 5:2)

This is still true. It is also still true that "we shall all be
changed in a moment, in the twinkling of an eye" (I
Corinthians 15:52). The trumpet that is said to herald the
raising of the dead is traditionally associated with the end
of the world and the Day of the Lord (Zephaniah 1:14-16;
Matthew 24:31; Revelation 8 and 9).

Paul is right to say that he is telling a mystery when
he prophesies the Second Coming. How do we live with
this expectation, which is certainly part of our faith? Surely
the answer is that we are in God's Kingdom now, as Paul
was when he was writing. So whenever Christ comes, it
will be a case of making visible to everybody what
already exists within us and within the Church. After all,
death is simply a move from one room to another in God's
Kingdom and that may well "come like a thief in the
night". This is not a cause for depression. It is wonderful
to be with Christ whatever befalls us, in this life or the
next.

Bible readings

- I Thessalonians 4:13-18 (We shall always be with the
  Lord)
- Malachi 3:13-18 (They shall be mine, says the Lord of
  hosts)

3. Your life is hid with Christ in God

*If then you have been raised with Christ, seek the things
that are above, where Christ is, seated at the right hand of
God. Set your minds on things that are above, not on things
that are on earth. For you have died, and your life is hid*

with Christ in God. When Christ who is our life appears,
then you also will appear with him in glory.

(Colossians 3:1-4)

Earlier in this letter to the Christians at Colossae Paul
has criticised some of the congregation for emphasising
rules about food, for worshipping angels, for claiming special visions and for undergoing meaningless ritual humilia-
tion (see 2:16-19). Paul wishes them instead to set their
minds on Christ and to "seek the things that are above", a
phrase which he repeats for emphasis. What does Paul
mean by "the things that are above"? He seems to be
referring to true Christian ideals and standards. In later
verses he outlines what is worst in earthly standards (verses
5-10), pulling no punches. He then goes into detail in
describing God's standards (verses 12-17), as always emphasising love.

Paul expresses his view of what the people should do by
once again using one of his favourite metaphors. If they
have been "raised with Christ" surely they must also have
died with him. In other words, they should be behaving in
Christlike ways, which some of them are obviously not
doing. Paul expresses this thought in a mysterious form by
saying that their lives are "hid with Christ in God". However, when Christ appears they will also "appear with him
in glory". The secrecy of the spiritual life in Christ seems
to be in Paul's mind. The depth of any person's relationship with God is hidden from the world. Outward manifestations are no sure guide to the true nature of a person's
spirituality. Yet the very hiddenness of this life in Christ is
a deep pool of joy which wells up in the everyday life of
the Christian. Those who have this secret relationship will
not behave according to the lowest earthly standards, but
according to the light of Christ which surrounds them.

Another way of interpreting Paul's thought is perhaps to
say that the true members of the Church are only known to
Christ and that they will be revealed when he appears in
glory because he will invite them to share in his glory. At

the same time, Christians who have died with Christ should have already risen with him in terms of the growth of their characters and that should be a present change, not a future one. The implication is that those who are practising insincere religion, that is those who "are puffed up without reason" (2:18), will not be part of the glory when Christ appears because they have not undertaken the first stage of dying and rising with Christ within themselves.

A further implication of Paul's thought is that Christ himself is in God. In verse 1 he also suggests that Christ is "at the right hand of God". Both of these statements are ways of saying that the risen and ascended Christ is part of the Godhead, indeed as he always has been, before, during and after the Incarnation. To reverse this, of course, one can say that God was in Christ reconciling the world to himself (see I Corinthians 5:19), which amounts to the same thing. God shows himself through Christ and Christ shows himself as God. This is an inspiring thought and Paul rightly states this truth as the reason for his exhortation of the people of Colossae to live up to their ideals.

This is surely one of those biblical passages which addresses itself directly to us and to Christians of all times and all places. The challenge is immediate. Have I died with Christ? Have I been raised with Christ? Am I living up to my ideals? Is my secret life with Christ in God a living reality? The alternative for us, if we have any pretensions at all of being Christians is not very attractive. As T.S. Eliot put it, we may then only be able to say:

> "We are the hollow men
> We are the stuffed men
> Leaning together."
>
> (*The Hollow Men*)

Why don't we instead, every morning and every evening, shout with inward joy: "I turn to Christ!" The transforming power of Christ is free and abundant. That is Paul's message, but we have to respond to what God offers.

Bible readings

– Amos 5:6-7 (Seek the Lord and live)
– Romans 2:6-11 (He will render to every man according
  to his works)

4. If anyone is in Christ he is a new creation

*From now on, therefore, we regard no one from a human
point of view; even though we once regarded Christ from a
human point of view, we regard him thus no longer. Therefore, if anyone is in Christ, he is a new creation; the old has
passed away, behold, the new has come.*

(II Corinthians 5:16-17)

In the new age inaugurated by the incarnation of Christ,
previous standards are no longer applicable. The human
viewpoint has completely changed. Even if Christ himself
was once "regarded from a human point of view" this is no
longer the case, because Christ has been revealed in his
true persona as the Son of God.

It is clear that the newly created human being, the
Christian of the new age, is a new person because he or she
is in Christ. Paul shows that the "love of Christ controls us"
(v. 14) because he has died for everyone. This all embracing love is in one sense potential, because obviously not
"everyone" is living consciously in the new age. Nevertheless, the work of reconciliation initiated by Christ has begun in the Church and continues through the members of
the Church because "the message of reconciliation" (v. 19)
has been entrusted to us. The word "us" includes the community of Corinthian Christians, and it also includes every
Christian congregation up to the present day and beyond,
until the work of reconciliation has been completed.

It is also clear that every newly created human being
living in Christ has not yet been completed, otherwise
the members of the Church would be perfect, which

manifestly they are not (cf. Philippians 3:12). This means that Christ's creative process is continuous in each individual as well as in the community. The word of Christ is a seed sown in the human soul, as the parable of the sower suggests (see Mark 4:1-20). When the soul is receptive the word grows and produces fruit up to a hundredfold. Even then, the creative process is not complete. It is doubtful if it will ever be complete in this world, unless Christ chooses to bring the reality of the kingdom of heaven to its fulfilment on earth.

The newly created human being, then, as far as we can tell, is in a special phase of growth, but will not be perfected until he (or she) puts on the heavenly body of the resurrection. This can scarcely be called the "fast lane", though it may lead to greater maturity. It is more like a slow lane in the sense that with spiritual growth comes a sense of eternity and the need for time and space to pray. So in worldly terms the growing life in the spirit may seem very slow indeed. As Edward Henry Bickersteth put it:

"Peace, perfect peace, in this dark world of sin?
The Blood of Jesus whispers peace within."
(Songs in the *House of Pilgrimage*)

Paul does say that "the old has passed away, behold the new has come" (v. 17 above). This may refer to the perspective of the new life in Christ that is burgeoning within. In some cases there is an explosion of light within the soul. With other people, visions of heaven are glimpsed as if, when the mist parts briefly, a beautiful valley appears momentarily in the dawn sunshine. And so it is that, despite our imperfections, each new day can bring new life and renewed vision. We do not have to live the old life because Christ will carry us through each new day until evening comes. We can borrow a little of eternity as we spend perhaps a little time in meditating on the works of the Lord, especially on his work within our souls. As the psalmist writes:

"... I think of thee upon my bed,
and meditate on thee in the watches of the night;
for thou hast been my help,
and in the shadow of thy wings I sing for joy."

(Psalm 63:6-7.

Bible readings

– Romans 5:12-17 (Adam, the type of one who was to come)
– Ephesians 4:17-24 (Put on the new nature)

5. United with him in a resurrection like his

For if we have been united with him in a death like his, we shall certainly be united with him in a resurrection like his. We know that our old self was crucified with him so that the sinful body might be destroyed, and we might no longer be enslaved to sin. For he who has died is freed from sin. For if we have died with Christ, we believe that we shall also live with him. For we know that Christ being raised from the dead will never die again; death no longer has dominion over him.

(Romans 6:5-9)

Yet again Paul makes the death and resurrection of Jesus very personal. Any real unity with Christ brings the will to crucify the old self, a process which frees us from sin; and if we have died with him, "we believe that we shall also live with him." "Living with Christ" seems to have a double meaning here, as it often does in Paul's thinking. There is the personal quality of the new life we shall have in the here and now when we accept Christ as Saviour. Then there is the resurrection life that awaits beyond this life.

The sinful body (literally "body of sin") in v. 6 may also

refer to the corporate group of all sinners as opposed to the corporate group of those living in Christ. This is not a black and white separation in the sense that Christians are entirely free from sin. Nor are sinners untouched by love and goodness. Yet, as the body of Christ grows through the Church, it would be expected that the total amount of love and goodness would grow and that the total amount of sin would diminish. The love of Christ is the leaven in the loaf and it is constantly working for change.

Paul associates the death of the old self with the sacrament of baptism (v. 3) and he actually claims that being baptised in Christ is being "baptised into his death". Paul's view of the sacrament is discussed elsewhere in the book, but it is worth noting now this association in Paul's mind between crucifying the self and accepting baptism. Of course, one of the effects of baptism is the washing away of sin (see Mark 1:4) and so Paul's line of thought is not surprising. What Paul does, however, is to highlight the importance of the inner life. The external sign of baptism is important, but without the internal change of repentance it would lose its true significance.

This is as true to today as it was for the early church. The custom of baptising infants is just as valid in this respect as the baptism of adults. When a baptised child makes a later commitment at first communion or confirmation, the internal meaning of the baptism is accepted. The effect of this commitment, according to Paul's reasoning, is that the Christian should be conscious from day to day of his or her death in Christ. New sins need to be crucified as the old have been. This also means that a spiritual resurrection may be a daily experience. Any true prayer life ought to contain this element.

Paul goes on to say that "death no longer has dominion over him". Christ having overcome human death with all its pain and anguish, Christ having risen gloriously on Easter day, Christ having re-ascended into heaven to take up again the fullness of the divine being, Christ having redrawn the boundaries of life for humankind – death has lost its power to threaten people and to inspire fear. This means that the gates of death are opened wide in a new understanding of a continuing richness of life, and it also means that the sins of all humankind have been overcome with love. It can be seen, then, that not only is this transformation within the experience of each individual, but that it is also a universal truth newly revealed. The signpost marked "death" has been rewritten as "change". Death is not an end but a beginning. This is true for the spiritual death of repentance and it is also true for the physical death at the apparent end of a human life. The result in either case is regeneration.

It is well known that a generator produces electrical power. God could be described as a generator because he produces creative power. This is what he did in the original creation. However, God is also a regenerator in the sense that he recreates what he has already created. This means that his creation is continuous. He is not an absent deity who started off the clock of the universe and then forgot about it. He not only upholds his creation, but he also redirects it, recycles it, if you like. In this way he works on the human soul without removing the freedom of that soul. He invites us to cooperate in our own continuous regeneration.

Bible readings

- II Corinthians 1:8-11 (God will deliver us again)
- Philippians 1:19-26 (My desire is to depart and be with Christ)

6. That I may know him and the power of his resurrection

Indeed I count everything as loss because of the surpassing worth of knowing Christ Jesus my Lord. For his sake I have

*suffered the loss of all things, and count them as refuse, in
order that I may gain Christ and be found in him, not
having a righteousness of my own, based on law, but that
which is through faith in Christ, the righteousness from
God that depends on faith; that I may know him and the
power of his resurrection, and may share his sufferings,
becoming like him in his death, that if possible I may attain
the resurrection from the dead.*

(Philippians 3:8-11)

Paul has not only crucified sin within himself, but he
has also given up a whole life style in order to serve God.
He has become a nomad without a permanent home; he
has given up any idea of getting married and having a
family (which to a Jew would be a great sacrifice); he has
virtually given up his very Jewishness, including his
family traditions (v. 5); he has given up the comforts of
ordinary life and taken on the hardships of being a persecuted, wandering preacher; he has given up his Roman
citizen's freedom to be a prisoner for the Lord's sake.
He can well say, without exaggeration: "Indeed I count
everything as loss because of the surpassing worth of knowing Christ Jesus."

Paul is often scornful about outward signs like circumcision which are valueless without the inner transformation
such signs are supposed to represent. Even his own circumcision he counts as loss for the sake of Christ. According to
Paul the true circumcision lies with the Christian Church
"who worship God in spirit, and glory in Christ Jesus, and
put no confidence in the flesh" (v. 3). In this discarding of
outward traditions he is following the principles of Christ's
teaching (Matthew 6:1-24). Yet, Paul does not boast that he
has already attained the certainty of resurrection with Christ.
He has his hope that if possible he may attain the resurrection from the dead (v. 11).

In the same way, any righteousness that he may possess
is "that which is through faith in Christ, the righteousness
from God that depends on faith" (v. 9). Those who criticise

Paul's principle of "justification through faith" or those who over emphasise it, often omit to mention that nobody else in Christian history could have demonstrated so fully by his deeds that he was God's instrument working in the world. It is impossible in Paul to separate faith from works. His faith was as big as the proverbial mountain and his works were no less conspicuous. It was because he wished to live close to Christ, to "share in his sufferings, becoming like him in his death" (v. 10), that he was able to give so much. It was in the power of Christ's resurrection that he lived each hour of each day.

Paul wished to share Christ's sufferings and certainly he suffered much at the hands of his enemies and from the rigours of travelling (see II Corinthians 11:23-29). In the end he paid the ultimate penalty of dying for his faith in Christ, though not on a cross as St Andrew and St Peter did, according to tradition. Paul did say that he would much rather be in heaven with Christ than continue to live his life on earth (Philippians 1:23). However, he also said, "But to remain in the flesh is more necessary on your account" (1:24), indicating that his duty was to work with might and main to convert the world to the Christian faith while he had life and breath.

This is a challenge to each of us. If we are serious about dying and rising with Christ in our daily lives, we ought to strive to be more like Paul in our commitment. It is a little depressing to try to compare ourselves with the great saints, but nevertheless, with the help of Christ we may achieve things which appear on the surface to be beyond our capabilities. Or, to take a slightly different view, every little helps: each small act of love, each word spoken in Christ's love, each thoughtful prayer, all help to build the Kingdom of God. Moreover, we have to start where we are. What can we do within our family, within our immediate neighbourhood, within the congregation of our church?

John Henry Newman lived a long and busy life. Like Paul he suffered persecution and his earthly pilgrimage was not smooth. However, he worked for the Lord in the light that was given to him. Some of his words may help us on our pilgrimage:

"May He support us all the day long, till the shades lengthen, and the evening comes, and the busy world is hushed, and the fever of life is over, and our work is done! Then in his mercy may He give us a safe lodging, and a holy rest, and peace at the last."

(Sermon on Wisdom and Innocence)

Many saints have followed Christ in hard times and good. They have crucified themselves in Christ and risen with him. Now they are in the great company of the saints in heaven, but no doubt they are still in some way working and praying for us. It is a comforting thought to feel that St Paul is still active on our behalf, especially through the organisations of which he is the patron saint.

Bible readings

– Ephesians 3:20-21 (The power at work within us)
– I Corinthians 5:8-13 (Fools for Christ's sake)

7. You are God's temple

Do you not know that you are God's temple and that God's Spirit dwells in you? If anyone destroys God's temple, God will destroy him. For God's temple is holy, and that temple you are.

(I Corinthians 3:16-17)

The idea that each of us is God's temple and the dwelling place of the Holy Spirit complements Paul's thinking in other passages about the personal nature of religion. In the sections above it has been seen that Paul feels the dying and risen Christ within himself and he suggests that Christ should be within each Christian. Here he changes the metaphor to conceive that the Spirit of God is within each of us.

Paul would be very familiar with the writings of the great Hebrew prophets and he would be aware of Jeremiah's view of real religion:

"I will put my law within them and I will write it upon their hearts; and I will be their God, and they shall be my people" (Jeremiah 31:33).

The thinking of other Old Testament prophets about the inner life of the spirit in true religion is not dissimilar to Jeremiah's (see Amos 5:21-24; Ezekiel 11:19). Paul takes this view a stage further. The true temple of God lies within each person. This would be a startling thought for the average Jewish person in the time of St Paul. For Jews the Jerusalem temple was the supreme holy place where God dwelt upon earth. It would also be a challenging thought to Gentiles who would be familiar with the idea that the gods dwelt in their temples, at least in their earthly manifestations.

It is even more challenging to think that God's temple is holy and therefore, as temples where God dwells, we should also be holy. The idea of striving for holiness and perfection goes back a long way in the priestly traditions (Leviticus 20:26); and Jesus takes up the thought in the Sermon on the Mount (Matthew 5:48). Of course, our Lord also spoke about God being within us in a very personal way:

"If a man loves me, he will keep my word, and my Father will love him, and we will come to him and make our home with him" (John:14:23).

It can be seen, then, that Paul is operating within a tradition in which religion is interpreted in very personal ways.

This should give us pause for thought in relation to the externals of our religious system. The externals exist to promote true religion, not to strangle it. The externals are good and helpful, but only if they reach the deepest parts of the inner life. To receive the sacraments is wonderful; but their effect may be dulled if the inward spirit is out of tune with the outward and visible sign. To kneel before a crucifix is helpful, because we perceive a meaningful image; but unless we crucify ourselves with Christ, as Paul suggests, the full impact of the image may be lost. Similarly, the resurrection is the world's greatest good news; but unless we feel ourselves risen with Christ each day, we are missing some of the glory.

The poet William Wordsworth was privileged to experience glimpses of heaven and to perceive that our true home is in heaven:

"But trailing clouds of glory do we come
From God, who is our home..."
(Ode: *Intimations of Immortality*)

In Paul's terms, God is around us and God upholds the whole of creation, but God is also within us. If we miss that, we miss the major part of our faith. True worship takes place in God's temple; God's love is in his temple; Christ and the Spirit dwell in his temple – and each Christian is that temple.

Bible readings

– Ephesians 2:19-22 (The household of God)
– Colossians 1:14-29 (The glory of this mystery which is Christ in you)

VI
Christians and the world

1. The Christian life

For the grace of God has appeared for the salvation of all men, training us to renounce irreligion and worldly passions, and to live sober, upright, and godly lives in this world, awaiting our blessed hope, the appearing of the glory of our great God and Saviour Jesus Christ, who gave himself for us to redeem us from all iniquity and to purify for himself a people of his own who are zealous for good deeds.
(Titus 2:11-14)

This is part of a section in which Paul bids Titus to teach "sound doctrine" (v. 1). Paul uses this phrase in other Pastoral Letters (cf. I Timothy 1:10; II Timothy 4:3). It is clear that Paul means rules of behaviour, rather than principles of theology, though as he often does, he relates his advice to his doctrine of God (v. 11).

In the passage quoted, Paul points out that it is the grace of God which teaches people to undertake discipline in their behaviour. Paul highlights the difference between those who forsake religion to be free to satisfy their worldly passions, and those who try "to live sober, upright and godly lives in this world..." (v. 12). In the previous paragraph Paul has detailed some of the categories of behaviour which are unacceptable for Christian people. These include: slander, drinking to excess, pilfering, irreverence and disobedience. Good aspects of behaviour which he mentions include: temperance, love, steadfastness, chastity, kindness, self control, integrity, soundness of speech and submissiveness.

In the preceding section Paul mentions five groups of people (vv. 1-10) and these are: older men and older women; younger men and younger women; and slaves. Paul, of course, accepts the custom of the day with regard to slavery. However, as the story of Philemon illustrates, Paul has an enlightened view within the limits of the then existing law. From Paul's general views it can be assumed that children were expected to be well behaved and obedient, though he doesn't mention children here (but see Ephesians 6:1-4).

Christ's work in redeeming us "from all iniquity" is emphasised here (v. 14). However, the positive side of the equation is that God's own people need to be pure and "zealous for good deeds". Paul never assumes that people can be good without God's help. Nevertheless, he does not absolve people from making the effort to be good (see I Timothy 4:7-16). God's grace is freely available, but that gift of grace needs to be used with energy and perseverance.

Paul certainly emphasises the importance of leadership. Titus is advised: "Declare these things; exhort and reprove with all authority" (v. 15). The difficulty in modern times is that authoritarianism is not popular. We tend to place the emphasis on individual freedom. Self discipline is seen as more valuable than enforced discipline. If Paul were alive today he might well agree with such an emphasis, but he would probably wish to insist upon sound moral training in the formative years, allowing more freedom as people were ready for it. This is a speculative view, of course, but Paul did ascribe great importance to personal responsibility (I Timothy 6:11-12) and love (I Corinthians 13) and it seems reasonable to suppose that he would try to obtain a creative balance between freedom and discipline within the community of the Church in today's world.

The big question for us is how we manage "to live sober, upright and godly lives in this world". "This world" must for us be our world, not Paul's world. Yet, Paul's advice is sound for all societies in all ages. What we need to do is to interpret his excellent advice so that we can apply his principles today. Certainly, the temptation to indulge in "worldly passions" and to ignore religion are very strong. Through the mass media we are bombarded constantly with images of violence and sexual licence. Some people rarely, if ever, enter the door of a religious building. However, God's message through Paul and other Biblical writers is clear. The Church needs to address these problems energetically.

This is a responsibility for each one of us, but we cannot preach to others if our own lives are in disorder. How, then, do we apply Paul's principles? Being "sober" surely doesn't mean not having fun. It rather means having a serious outlook on life when the chips are down. Being "upright" surely means loving our neighbour and sticking to the moral rules of the Bible, bearing in mind that love occasionally supersedes the rules. Being "godly" in our approach to life may be subject to differing interpretations, but, at the very least, it must mean taking God seriously in our main decisions and actions. Recognising temptation when it comes and resisting it are part of the Christian ethos. The First Letter of Peter makes a similar point:

"Be sober, be watchful. Your adversary the devil prowls around like a roaring lion, seeking someone to devour. Resist him, firm in your faith, knowing that the same experience of suffering is required of your brotherhood throughout the world" (I Peter 5:8-9).

Bible readings

- II Corinthians 6:14–7:1 (What fellowship has light with darkness?)
- Ephesians 5:1-11 (Be imitators of God)

2. Hold fast what is good

Be at peace among yourselves. And we exhort you, brethren, admonish the idlers, encourage the faint hearted, help the weak, be patient with them all. See that none of you repays evil for evil, but always seek to do good to one another and to all. Rejoice always, pray constantly, give thanks in all circumstances; for this is the will of God in Christ Jesus for you. Do not quench the Spirit, do not despise prophesying, but test everything; hold fast what is good, abstain from every form of evil.

(I Thessalonians 5:13b-22)

Essentially Paul is here speaking to the Christian community, but his words do have more general import. On the one hand, he is advising Church members to be at peace among themselves, but he is also exhorting them to put aside the evils of the world and to "hold fast what is good".

Relationships within the congregation ought to take account of the weaker members. Some need encouragement because they are "faint hearted". Those who won't pull their weight need some straight talking. Those who are weak, either morally or physically, need help. However, in dealing with all of these people Paul suggests that patience is essential. This is surely good advice for all Christian groups. Indeed, in any community where people work closely together this advice is helpful.

As usual, though, Paul is very positive. The best way to have good relationships within a community, especially within the Church, is to follow the golden rule of not repaying evil with evil. Instead of following the revenge seeking impulse, it is much more constructive to "do good to one another and to all". This moves the perspective into the wider community. The same rule applies to all human relationships as applies within the congregation. Do good to all.

The heart of Church life is Christ himself. Paul reminds

his readers of this and in doing so states three wonderful principles for a happy and creative spiritual life: "Rejoice always, pray constantly, give thanks in all circumstances; for this is the will of God in Christ Jesus for you" (vv. 16-18). We certainly have much to rejoice about. As John Keble wrote:

"Come, very Sun of truth and love,
Come in thy radiance from above,
And shed the Holy Spirit's ray
On all we think or do today."

When all the glories of the Gospel are considered, each day should surely be approached with a heart full of joy.

We also have much to pray about, especially if we consider that everything we think or speak or do may be a prayer offered to God. At the same time, there are occasions of deeper private prayer, and at these times of daily discipline the spirit is renewed and restored. Even our Lord himself felt the need to go to quiet places to pray (see Matthew 14:23).

Also, we have a great deal to give thanks for. Paul emphasises that we should give thanks "in all circumstances". He certainly had his difficult times such as when he was in prison, when he was beaten and when he was shipwrecked. Yet, he seems to say, we should give thanks even at those times when life seems grim. This may be difficult if we have lost a close friend or relative, for example. On the other hand, the reality of Christ "crosses" through these situations and it is wonderful to know that nothing, absolutely nothing, can "separate us from the love of Christ" (Romans 8:35).

The advice not "to quench the Spirit" seems strange. It is quite obvious that no human being could quench the Spirit of God. Probably what Paul is referring to is manifestations of the Spirit in the form of speaking in tongues. This view is supported by the request not to despise prophesying. However, the cautious Paul insists that everything should be tested. Certainly he advises discrimination in these matters, though he is more in favour of prophesying than of speaking in tongues (I Corinthians 14:1-5). Nevertheless, the Thessalonians are told not to "quench the Spirit", so Paul obviously feels that religious experience enriches through many channels. Perhaps the lesson for us is that we should not readily condemn religious practices which are not familiar to us, but that we should use caution in assessing them.

Bible readings

– Colossians 2:1-7 (Abounding in thanksgiving)
– Galatians 5:22-26 (Walking by the Spirit)

3. Shine as lights in the world

Do all things without grumbling or questioning, that you may be blameless and innocent, children of God without blemish in the midst of a crooked and perverse generation, among whom you shine as lights in the world, holding fast the word of life, so that in the day of Christ I may be proud that I did not run in vain or labour in vain.

(Philippians 2:14-16)

To describe the faithful as shining like lights in the world inevitably reminds us of the image of Jesus as the light of the world. By contrast, Paul describes the world in general as "crooked and perverse"; in other words as a place of darkness where the light of Christ in the Church gleams like a beacon.

This exhortation follows the wonderful description of Christ as the one who, though in God's form, emptied himself and became a servant. The least Christians can do, in following Christ's light, is to "do all things without grumbling or questioning". Paul is probably referring to the call of duty, which should lead us to perform many acts of service for others. These we should do cheerfully and without a great fuss. It was William Wordsworth who called duty the "stern daughter of the voice of God", and certainly Paul is being quite stern here in his reminder. However, love is never far from Paul's thought and duty in his eyes would not be cold and unbending, but full of warmth and love. His reminder has a gentle aspect in that he refers to his readers as " my beloved" (v. 12). He also emphasises that doing one's duty, even if it leads to death in Christ's service, is cause for gladness and rejoicing (v. 17). Paul seems to be very much aware that his own life is in constant danger.

To do things without questioning is difficult for people today. Paul lived in a more authoritarian age than ours. We like to know why we are doing things. We challenge authority and demand answers. The authority of both State and Church are often called in question. Before we commit ourselves to a cause we like to be certain of the ground rules. At the same time, many people today, both inside and outside the Church, commit themselves deeply to self-less causes when they are convinced these are right and good. People work for the physically handicapped, lend their skills to under privileged countries, organise convoys of food and medical supplies to areas of need. There are some wonderful people around, even "in the midst of a crooked and perverse generation".

Perhaps Paul recognises the need to question one's con-science or one's principles at certain times when he says "work out your own salvation in fear and trembling" (v. 12). At the same time he says that God is at work in us, and it is in this context that we have to work out our salvation. This seems to point to individual responsibility in the faith. Ultimately each of us is alone before God.

Having recognised our need to question authority be-fore commitment, it is nevertheless true that when we have committed ourselves to Christ there may be certain things we should do without "grumbling or questioning".

We commit ourselves to a loving way of life, to helping others, to being servants within and beyond the Christian community. When our consciences tell us clearly that a certain course is the right one, then perhaps we should follow it without grumbling or questioning even if difficulties arise. For example, if a man decides to work for a charitable group as part of his duty to God and his fellow human beings, then he accepts that he has to make sacrifices of time and energy and finances. This commitment accepted, he does not then grumble and question all the time, not at any rate if he is in the service of Christ.

We are not left without support when we commit ourselves. If we "hold fast the word of life", then we have a life line to God. This "holding fast" is really making Christ our anchor in life. This cannot be done by a casual Church commitment. It means pursuing a discipline of prayer and worship. It means linking in to the Christian community with all its human faults. The undergirding power of the Church is the Holy Spirit and it is in this power that we have our strength and courage. To become children of God means we have to live in the Spirit, to live with Christ as our brother, to turn for help each day to God our Father. Even if we do live "in the midst of a crooked and perverse generation", we should remember the words of our Lord himself:

"In the world you have tribulation; but be of good cheer, I have overcome the world" (John 16:33).

Bible readings

– II Corinthians 9:6-9 (God loves a cheerful giver)
– II Corinthians 4:1-6 (The light of the gospel of the glory of Christ)

4. Do everything in the name of the Lord Jesus

Put on then, as God's chosen ones, holy and beloved, compassion, kindness, lowliness, meekness, and patience, forbearing one another and, if one has a complaint against another, forgiving each other; as the Lord has forgiven you, so you also must forgive. And above all these, put on love, which binds everything together in perfect harmony. And let the peace of Christ rule in your hearts, to which indeed you were called in the one body. And be thankful. Let the word of Christ dwell in you richly, teach and admonish one another in all wisdom, and sing psalms and hymns and spiritual songs with thankfulness in your hearts to God. And whatever you do, in word or deed, do everything in the name of the Lord Jesus, giving thanks to God the Father through him.

(Colossians 3:12-17)

This is a very positive view of the ethical side of the Christian vocation which places love is at the very centre of life. Love is the conductor which brings perfect harmony to the whole of the new nature which the Christian puts on after he has died with Christ. Those aspects of our behaviour which are put to death with the old nature are described vividly by Paul in the previous paragraph, in which he pulls no punches. Paul certainly believed in straight talking, but he rarely if ever leaves the negative commandments hanging in the air. He usually turns the attention of the reader from what he ought not to do to what he ought to do. This fits in with Paul's view of the law, that it is useful for telling us about wrongdoing and sin, but that it cannot of itself save us (Romans 3:20-26). Only the love of God in Christ can do that (I Corinthians 13). When such love fills us to the brim we are then in a position to put Christ's teaching into practice, to be his instruments for changing the world. This is true even if each of us contributes only a little. Yet some people are required to give all that they possess and all that they are in the service of Christ.

As well as reminding his readers that they have been chosen by God, Paul accompanies the invitation to put on Christ with the tactful assumption that the members of the Christian community at Colossae are "holy and beloved" (v.12). To be told you are a "saint" (an alternative translation) means you are more likely to act like one. This is the reverse of giving a dog a bad name. If somebody is given a good name he or she will usually try to live up to the reputation ascribed to him or her. A good reputation is a kind of armour, because to lose that reputation by bad behaviour is to lose an important part of one's self identity. However, we have to remember that Christ made himself of no reputation (Philippians 2:7) in order to save the world. Similarly, he associated with despised groups of people in order to show God's love to them (Luke 4:16-21). Sometimes the demands of the gospel may lead Christians to sacrifice their reputations or even their lives.

Paul's list of Christian virtues gives a paradigm for all Christians in all ages. Compassion, kindness, lowliness, meekness, patience, forbearance, forgiveness and love are the qualities we should strive to have. If to those characteristics are added the peace of Christ and the word of Christ within the heart, as Paul suggests, then putting on the new nature would transform us through and through.

To perform all our words and actions in the name of Christ is what we should aim for. This should mean that no corner of our existence is separated from Christ. The people we meet at work or in the pub, as well as those we meet at church, are all within the ambit of God's love shining through us. When we go shopping or do the housework, or dig the garden, we should be acting in Christ's name. After all, Jesus himself was a carpenter and Paul was a tentmaker (see Acts 18:3). Not infrequently, in the course of our daily round, we come across someone who is unhappy for some reason. Watching for opportunities to help such people is part of Christ's work. Even to say a prayer for someone who is obviously in some kind of need may bring a great blessing to that person. Prayers are always heard and are always responded to in some way, though we may not necessarily be able to see the response in an immediate sense.

Yet again Paul sees the worship of the Christian community as an integral part of the action of that community. To "sing psalms and hymns and spiritual songs with thankfulness" in our hearts, is to bring us the joy of relating directly to God, which in turn will strengthen us in spirit to go out into the world again. Indeed, to take our worship out into the world may also be the right thing to do in the right context. Paul certainly did this himself (see Acts 16:13) and charismatic Christians like St Francis and John Wesley have done likewise. It was Wesley who wrote, "I look upon all the world as my parish" (Journal for June 11th 1739). All the world is certainly Christ's domain and if we receive the call to obey our Lord's command to "go therefore and make disciples of all nations" (Matthew 28:19) we should not hesitate to use whatever gifts we have to follow the call. Paul himself saw his mission as the conversion of the world and it is largely due to his initial work that the Roman Empire eventually became Christian under Constantine. That kind of progress in furthering God's Kingdom can only take place through the agency of God's servants in the world, and only if they show the face of Christ in a way that the world can understand. Principally, this will be through the medium of love.

Bible readings

– II Corinthians 6:1-10 (Now is the day of salvation)
– I Thessalonians 1:2-8 (The labour of love)

5. Do not be conformed to this world

I appeal to you, therefore, brethren, by the mercies of God, to present your bodies as a living sacrifice, holy and ac-

*ceptable to God, which is your spiritual worship. Do not be
conformed to this world but be transformed by the renewal
of your mind, that you may prove what is the will of God,
what is good and acceptable and perfect.*

(Romans 12:1-2)

These verses form the introduction to a whole section
on the Christian way of life. In the first part of the letter
Paul has demonstrated how the new life in Christ comes
from God himself. Now he proceeds to explain what the
new life involves in terms of commitment.

Paul gives the first requirement of the Christian life as a
complete surrender of the whole self to God. First, the
body is to be given to God "as a living sacrifice". In Paul's
time the Jewish temple was the place where sacrifices were
offered to God. Paul had been educated within a religious
system where the regular offering of animals in sacrifice
was important. Mary and Joseph offered the conventional
sacrifice when they presented Jesus in the temple (Luke
2:22-24). Jesus, however, later presented himself as the
Passover lamb and as the atonement sacrifice to supersede
the whole sacrificial system. (In fact, the Jewish people
continued to sacrifice in the Jerusalem temple until it was
destroyed in 70 AD.)

What Paul is suggesting to the Romans is that they too
should present themselves as living sacrifices. Of course,
when an animal sacrifice was made in the temple the animal was killed. The difference in the personal sacrifice of a
Christian is that it is a living sacrifice, a sacrifice of the
whole person for the future life in this world and the next.
At the same time, Paul often drew a parallel between our
Lord's crucifixion (his sacrifice of himself) with the crucifixion of the self (each Christian's sacrifice in Christ) (see
Romans 6:5 for example). In this way, the sinful body is
sacrificed so that the new, risen body may serve Christ as a
sacrifice "holy and acceptable to God".

Paul's thought on the Christian body is developed further in verses 4-5. The whole Church becomes the body,

and each member of the Church is part of that body. Here Paul says that "we, though many, are one body in Christ". The Eucharistic body of Christ is probably also in Paul's mind. What Paul reveals to us in a brilliant merging of metaphors is that the sacrificed body of Christ incorporates the sacrifices of our own bodies so that the Church, in effect, is the body of Christ upon earth, still working, still bringing God's word to the world.

Returning to verse 2, Paul goes on to say that our minds should be transformed and renewed and that we should "not be conformed to this world". The Greek word translated "world" refers to the present age, the time based world in which we live. Jesus himself uses the word of the resurrection time (Luke 20:35) and the age to come (Mark 10:30). Paul is suggesting then, that as well as sacrificing our bodies in an act of true worship, we should also change the direction of our thoughts so that we can "prove" (or test) the will of God. To "prove" the will of God seems to mean that in our actions we should test ourselves out against the criteria revealed in our faith; that we should strive for "what is good and acceptable and perfect"; and that we hope in this way to conform with God's will, rather than with the ways of the world.

What does this mean for us in our "age". The ground rules are very much the same as they were in Paul's time. As William Wordsworth put it:

"The world is too much with us now; late and soon
Getting and spending, we lay waste our powers..."
                                        (Miscellaneous Sonnets)

We certainly do a lot of "getting and spending" and a lot of "wasting", not only of our own potential, but also of the world's resources. Sadly, we "conform to this world" much too frequently. An antidote to the resulting despair of ourselves and the world in which we live is to take Paul's advice and present ourselves to God as "living sacrifices". God is changing the world, but he has chosen us to do the job for him. It is of no use squirming in our seats and saying, "He can't mean me!" He does mean "me", and each of us has the possibility of meeting Christ at the cross, which may prove to be the major junction in our lives.

Bible readings

– Romans 8:28-30 (Conformed to the image of his Son)
– Ephesians 1:3-10 (Holy and blameless before him)

6. The love of money is the root of all evils

There is great gain in godliness with contentment; for we brought nothing into the world, and we cannot take anything out of the world; but if we have food and clothing, with these we shall be content. But those who desire to be rich fall into temptation, into a snare, into many senseless and hurtful desires that plunge men into ruin and destruction. For the love of money is the root of all evils; it is through this craving that some have wandered away from the faith and pierced their hearts with many pangs.

(I Timothy 6:6-10)

Paul is here criticising those teachers who wish to show that godliness is a means of gain (see the preceding v. 5). Paul agrees that godliness is certainly a means of gain, but then goes on to show that he does not refer to material gain. Contentment is the key to happiness. If we remember that we leave this world as we came into it, with no personal possessions, then we shall have a sense of reality. Paul accepts the future life of the resurrection as a matter of faith (v. 12) and it is fair to deduce from what he says that he believes the things that will be valuable in the future life will be "righteousness, godliness, faith, love, steadfastness, gentleness" (v. 11).

There are, of course, some basic essentials for life. Paul

mentions in particular food and clothing and suggests that if we have sufficient of these then we ought to be content. In his own life his requirements were obviously very simple. He was used to roughing it on his travels and he was ready to take people as he found them (Acts 16:15; I Thessalonians 1:9). Today perhaps we regard too many things as essential for a happy life. The washing machine, the television, the vacuum cleaner, the freezer and many other household goods have become accepted as the norm. If Paul were alive today he would possibly say that these things are all right in their place, but that we shouldn't believe that they are essential to life's main purposes. More probably, he would argue that everybody should have a fair share of the world's resources and that some people have too many possessions.

In the often misquoted verse 10 he condemns the *love* of money as the root of all evils. This is generally taken to be a well known Greek proverb. It fits in well with Paul's argument which is that the desire to be rich leads people into many snares and temptations. Sometimes people even ruin their lives by their pursuit of riches. Those who become rich are not always happy. The couple who win a large sum on the football pools or in a lottery may find that their new perspective on life ruins their old friendships. The person who makes his sole object in life the pursuit of wealth may spend so much time working that he misses out on all the really important things like love and companionship. The person who cheats and steals to become rich may find eventually that his misdeeds catch up with him.

According to Paul some people "have wandered away from the faith" on account of the love of money. The result is that they pierce their own hearts with many painful experiences. Riches do not sit well with Christianity, though to be sure, some rich people are good church people, mainly because they have achieved a right perspective. Their wealth may not be the most important factor in their lives. They may indeed give generously to many good causes. It is when money becomes a god that people get into difficul-

113

ties. This may not be immediately apparent, but the fact is that life is short and ultimately every single person has to face up to the abandonment of all that they outwardly possess. If money has been at the centre of a person's life, he may find that he has no inner resources to face a real crisis like the death of a loved one or the discovery that he himself has cancer.

When we consider Christ's sacrifice of himself at such a young age and so selflessly; when we think of the simple life he led beside Galilee and in the hills around Nazareth; when we think of the ways in which he helped the people he met through his untiring service; when we think of the spiritual riches he has brought to the world – we can only agree with Isaac Watts when he wrote:

"When I survey the wondrous Cross,
On which the Prince of glory died,
My richest gain I count but loss
And pour contempt on all my pride."

Bible readings

- Matthew 6:19-21 (Treasure in heaven)
- Colossians 2:1-7 (All the treasures of wisdom and knowledge)

7. God is faithful, and he will not let you be tempted beyond your strength

Therefore let anyone who thinks that he stands take heed lest he fall. No temptation has overtaken you that is not common to man. God is faithful, and he will not let you be tempted beyond your strength, but with the temptation will also provide the way of escape, that you may be able to endure it.

(I Corinthians 10:12-13)

This passage follows one of the most serious warnings against sin that Paul ever wrote in any of his extant letters. He warns that the reward at the end of life, the imperishable wreath of everlasting life, may be lost through indiscipline (9:24-27). Then he reminds his readers that the Israelites had gone through a form of baptism "in the cloud and in the sea" (10:2) and that they had eaten supernatural food and drunk supernatural drink (v. 3). Nevertheless, many of the Israelites who had possessed these advantages had been "destroyed by the Destroyer" (v. 10).

The parallel for their Church would have been clear to the congregation of Corinth. They too had been baptised; they too had eaten supernatural food (in the Eucharist); and they too could be destroyed by their own disobedience of God. "Therefore," writes Paul, "let anyone who thinks that he stands take heed lest he fall" (v. 12). This is a salutary warning for all of us. Temptation comes in many forms, some of them notoriously attractive. Even Jesus himself underwent a series of temptations (see Matthew 4:1-11). The Lord's Prayer, taught to the disciples and in turn to us, contains the petition, "Lead us not into temptation".

God gave us a sense of humour in addition to the capacity to be tempted. Sometimes our ability to laugh helps us to put things in perspective, though Oscar Wilde's advice on dealing with temptation is probably over the top for most Christians. He wrote, "The only way to get rid of a temptation is to yield to it" (Picture of Dorian Gray). At the same time it can be helpful to distinguish between temptations which may prove mildly hurtful to ourselves and those which are potentially very hurtful to others. It is one thing to eat too many chocolates, but it is quite another to steal or to murder or to commit adultery. Fortunately most of our temptations do not come into the latter categories. Yet, there are other more frequent temptations which are potentially damaging to ourselves or others. For example, there is the temptation not to do anything when somebody manifestly needs help. The story of the Good Samaritan illustrates that temptation very well (see Luke 10:25-37).

Some Christians may find a whole range of temptations which, if yielded to, will draw them away from their faith and from the Church. Friends who are not church members may lead us into pleasant social situations, which then lead us into not attending church as regularly as previously. Television may prove to be our downfall because we gradually succumb to standards which are not church standards. Work may have its demands, together with a desire for promotion or a larger salary and the temptation may be to focus on work instead of on God. A whole range of leisure activities may become of intense interest, and why not? Golf, weekend walking, fishing, horse racing, drinking and lunching with friends are all very engaging pursuits. However, they may offer temptations to give up our basic prayer discipline or to abandon some of our church connections. These things are not wrong in themselves. In fact, they are part of life's wonderful and interesting tapestry. Perhaps one of the greatest temptations is to have little interest in anything, to let faith die of apathy. What we probably have to do is to ensure we get the balance of our lives right. If God is at the centre of everything we do then all should be well.

Paul does make the point that all human beings are in the same boat as far as temptation is concerned. To be tempted is part of being human. Yet, writes Paul, "God is faithful, and he will not let you be tempted beyond your strength" (v. 13). As often, with St Paul, an exact interpretation of what he means is difficult. However, he possibly means that if people are living prayerfully, then God will be at hand in times of temptation. On the other hand, if people have turned their backs on God he may choose to allow them to learn by bitter experience. To some extent all of us must do that.

Some temptations are difficult to endure. Paul seems to recognise this when he allows that God may provide a "way of escape". This is encouraging, if rather cryptic. It would be acceptable to translate the Greek as "a way out" (Jerusalem Bible), which gives a slightly different nuance. Although we may not be able to escape completely from a temptation, God will provide a way out of the situation, whatever it may be. Perhaps each person has one supreme temptation, among many others he may experience in life. Suppose, for example, a man found that he was so hooked on computer games that he couldn't find the time to do essential things in the home and was often absent from work because of his addiction. If he prayed sincerely about his temptation, God might well provide a way out of his difficulty. He could meet a new friend who managed to guide him in the right direction or his wife might become pregnant for the first time. In the latter case he might be persuaded to sell all his computer software for the sake of the baby. What may seem trivial and unlikely to one person may be a deadly serious to another. To give another example, a woman who was tempted to commit suicide because of her drug addiction might be directed by a friend, first to the Samaritans and then to a clinic.

All of us need God's help. "There but for the grace of God go I," is a thought worth preserving when we are tending to be judgemental.

Bible readings

– Galatians 6:1-5 (Look to yourself, lest you too be tempted)
– I Thessalonians 3:1-5 (Established in the faith)

8. Think about these things

Finally, brethren, whatever is true, whatever is honourable, whatever is just, whatever is pure, whatever is lovely, whatever is gracious, if there is any excellence, if there is anything worthy of praise, think about these things.

(Philippians 4:8)

Paul's capacity to introduce gems of philosophy and religious wisdom into passages which are essentially about mundane matters is quite astonishing. Chapter Four of the letter to Philippi is about healing relationships (v. 2), about appeals to work hard (v. 3), and about thanks for gifts received from the congregation (vv. 10-19). Among these everyday concerns Paul introduces several immortal verses which have captured the imaginations of Christians and others over the centuries. In verse 4 he writes, "Rejoice in the Lord always; again I will say Rejoice." These words express the inner lining of a worshipping community with wonderful resonance.

Then in verse 7 Paul gives promise of a blessing in words which are so mysterious and beautiful that they express the relationship between God and his people in a never to be forgotten, poetic nutshell: "And the peace of God, which passes all understanding, will keep your hearts and minds in Christ Jesus."

Coming then to a summary of some of the highest ideals of the Christian community or, indeed, of the human race as a whole, Paul writes a final appeal to the Philippians to aim high in their attitudes to the world and each other. This is verse 8, the passage quoted above. Truth, honour, justice, purity, loveliness, grace, excellence, praiseworthy things – are listed by Paul as signposts for the development of Christian character. This, of course, is after he has given the congregation warnings about "evil workers" and "enemies of the cross of Christ" (see Chapter 3:2; 3:18-19).

It would not have been surprising if someone like Plato had written these words. The ideals Paul expresses are universals. Yet all the concepts appear in the Old Testament. However, whether Paul received his inspiration from the Jewish scriptures or from Greek philosophy is immaterial. Probably there are elements of both sources in his thinking. He certainly knew the scriptures inside out (Acts 22:3) and he was familiar with Greek literature (Acts 17:28). That is why he was the ideal person to be an apostle to the Gentiles.

Human ideals challenge us to try to touch the stars. We cannot often reach them. However, to strive to live by ideals brings out the best in the human character. Paul knows that perfectly well when he invites the Philippians to "think about these things". To try to live by the truth means not only searching for the great truths, but also that we attempt to avoid hypocrisy and the many self deceptions we are tempted to hide behind.

To pursue "whatever is honourable" is to be serious minded in our approach to life. In fact, the Greek word used by Paul he uses elsewhere to indicate serious-mindedness (see I Timothy 3:8; Titus 2:2). This includes the implications of the English word "honourable", meaning that we ought to do honour to our selves and to Christ by pursuing serious intentions in our lives.

"Whatever is just" could equally well be translated as "whatever is right". This means living according to the moral standards revealed to us in the Bible and, of course, this includes striving for justice for all members of the community, whether we are thinking of the Christian fellowship or the broader community in which we live.

"Whatever is pure" possibly refers to sincerity of motive, though Paul may also have had in mind the idea of holiness of character. However, earlier in the letter he uses an allied Greek word to refer to sincerity (Philippians 1:17). Of course Paul is undoubtedly aware of ambiguities in language and no doubt he often intends the full range of meanings in a word. Certainly, purity of heart and mind in relation both to God and other people is a quality Christians ought to acquire.

"Whatever is lovely" is not easy to interpret. The Greek word is rare and is an offshoot of the word for "love". The English "lovely" often means "pleasant" or "beautiful". However the Greek word might literally mean "from love" (or even "towards love") suggesting that "worthy of love" or even "lovingness" might be better translations. So if we think of things worthy of love, we may think of God himself and the beauties of his creation, or of people, especially when they are at their best (though not excluding them when they are at their worst). At the same time, "lovingness" implies an attitude within ourselves which is expressing love in all kinds of ways.

119

The words translated "whatever is gracious", according to a literal translation of the Greek, would refer to things which are of "good report". Possibly "having a good reputation" gives a reasonable interpretation. This could, at a stretch, be included in the nuances of the English word "gracious", which has a whole range of meanings.

The Greek word for "excellent" is used in the Bible to speak of supreme moral virtue or goodness, either of God (cf. II Peter 1:3) or of people (cf. II Peter 1:5). So Paul is most likely exhorting the people of Philippi to be virtuous in character and behaviour. At the same time, excellence in the general sense is worth aiming for. If we are doing all things for Christ then we should endeavour to produce the highest possible standards in all that we attempt.

To see things as "worthy of praise" means making judgements, but according to what standards? Surely according to the ideals Paul has just been outlining. Of course, we give praise to God, but we also praise people's achievements or their characters. We ought to remember also that a word of praise may inspire someone to do great things. Conversely, if people are never praised or if they are subjected constantly to criticism, they may well give up some good activity.

Finally, we ought to remember that ideals unrelated to the "nitty gritty" of life are not worth much. We have already seen that Paul gives his wonderful advice to real people facing the kinds of problems we face today. Let us pursue ideals, by all means, but let us try to change the world as we do so. That is what ideals are for. To follow Christ is to follow an ideal, but Christ is also involved in the day to day problems of the world. The Kingdom of God is an ideal, but it can only be built upon earth by human hands.

Bible readings

– II Timothy 2:20-26 (A vessel for noble use)
– Philippians 1:9-11 (That you may approve what is excellent)

VII
Living by the Spirit

1. The fruit of the Spirit

But the fruit of the Spirit is love, joy, peace, patience, kindness, goodness, faithfulness, gentleness, self-control; against such there is no law. And those who belong to Christ Jesus have crucified the flesh with its passions and desires. If we live by the Spirit let us also walk by the Spirit. Let us have no self-conceit, no provoking of one another, no envy of one another.

(Galatians 5:22-26)

According to Paul the life of the Spirit is opposed to the life of the flesh. He lists the works of the flesh in the previous section (19-21). Of course, "sins of the flesh" include all wrongdoings due to our human frailty. Some of these are very much related to the "flesh", but others in Paul's list are more related to the mind and the spirit (for example, enmity and selfishness). Jesus also lists sins, those things that come "out of the heart of man" (Mark 7:21-23) and it is not surprising that the two lists have much in common. But like Jesus, Paul puts more emphasis on love and other Christian virtues than he does on sin. In fact, the first virtue on Paul's list above is "love".

Paul has already made the point earlier in the letter to the Galatians that they have received the Spirit (3:2). He emphasises there that the Spirit does not come by means of the law. Then he says in the passage under discussion that "there is no law" against the fruits of the Spirit; and he says in previous verses (vv. 17-18): "For the desires of the flesh are against the Spirit, and the desires of the Spirit are against the flesh; for these are opposed to each other, to prevent you from doing what you would. But if you are led by the Spirit you are not under the law." It almost seems sometimes that Paul equates sin with the law, but of course he means that the law informs us about sin (see Romans 3:20).

One of the main themes of Paul's letter is that neither being a Jew nor being a Gentile is especially relevant in the context of "faith working through love" (5:6). He is very scathing about those who are insisting that circumcision is necessary to be a follower of Christ (5:2-3 and 5:12). In opposition to the slavery of the law and circumcision, Paul emphasises the call to freedom (5:13) and that freedom is life in the Spirit. The fruits of life in the Spirit represent some of the traditional Christian virtues. The list is obviously not exhaustive, because Paul does not include "hope" for example, one of the three great virtues he refers to in I Corinthians 13.

It is one thing to say that the law does not legislate against the Christian virtues. It is quite another to persuade people to display the sort of character which is based on the fruits of the Spirit as described by Paul. No doubt we could all mention one person we know who is loving, or another who is joyful, or another who is gentle, but how many people do we know who portray in full the Christian virtues listed? Possibly not very many. However, that is no cause for despair. The virtues exist to inspire us. Moreover, if people are living consciously in the Spirit, no doubt they will begin to acquire loving attitudes and to behave accordingly – as well as to begin to develop some of the other virtues on the list. At the same time, they will start to leave behind the sins listed by Paul as "works of the flesh" (vv. 19-21). Like Rome, the kingdom of heaven upon earth will not be built in a day and neither will the citizens of the kingdom bear all the fruits of the Spirit in one season.

Paul gives a reminder in vv. 25-26 that living by the Spirit means walking by the Spirit. In other words we ought to practise what we preach. Then, as he usually does, Paul roots his comments in the real situation in which the Galatians find themselves. He identifies some of the specific causes of dissension among the congregation. "Self conceit" often goes along with ignoring the other person's viewpoint. Deliberately "provoking one another" is definitely not among the fruits of the Spirit and people ought to stop stirring up cauldrons of hate. "Envy of one another" is often the reason why people get into arguments. Paul is saying the equivalent of, "Cool it, for goodness sake!"

Paul goes on in the subsequent chapter to give further advice on how the Christian ought to behave. One of the outstanding sayings, which supports what he has written about the "fruits of the Spirit" is "Bear one another's burdens, and so fulfil the law of Christ" (6:2).

Each one of us is challenged each day to endeavour to bear fruits of the Spirit. This is not possible without the guidance of the Spirit and without the help of our Lord himself. It would be a dismal time indeed if we were to walk without the Spirit. Paul would no doubt have approved of this verse by E. Hatch as good advice on how to walk with the Spirit:

"Breathe on me, Breath of God,
Fill me with life anew,
That I may love what thou dost love,
And do what thou wouldst do."

Bible readings

- II Corinthians 6:1-8 (The weapons of righteousness)
- Romans 14:17-19 (Peace and joy in the Holy Spirit)

2. Freedom and glory in the Spirit

Now the Lord is the Spirit, and where the Spirit of the Lord is, there is freedom. And we all, with unveiled face, beholding the glory of the Lord, are being changed into his likeness from one degree of glory to another; for this comes from the Lord who is the Spirit.

(II Corinthians 3:17-18)

Paul states here quite categorically that "the Lord is the Spirit". What is not clear is whether "Lord" refers to God or to Christ. Paul certainly refers to Jesus as Lord elsewhere, as in the Grace (cf. II Corinthians 13:14). On the other hand, the discussion about Moses and the veil in the preceding verses may indicate that in Paul's mind it is God who is Spirit. At the end of verse 18 the RSV translation above says "...for this comes from the Lord who is the Spirit." However, there are several possible translations for the Greek and this makes interpretation difficult.

It may help to clarify the issue to comment upon the reference to Moses and the veil. The Book of Exodus tells the story of how Moses used to speak with God and how, when he came back, his face shone. The people were afraid of Moses because of this strange phenomenon, so he took to wearing a veil, except when he was speaking with God (Exodus 34:29-35). Paul is making the point that the new splendour of the covenant in Christ far surpasses the old splendour of the Mosaic covenant. However, Christians dare to look at the glory of the Lord with unveiled face, in contrast to the Jews who dare not lift the veil from the ark which contained the scrolls of scripture. This is similar to the present day custom of veiling the reserved sacrament. Of course, the exposition of the sacrament, which some branches of the Church practise, would support Paul's argument. The main point of comparison though, is that the minds of Jewish people, according to Paul, are veiled and their minds are hardened against seeing the truth in Christ.

The key statement in the discussion is that "only through

Christ is it (the veil) taken away" (v. 14). The contrast, then, is that "whenever Moses is read a veil lies over their minds; but when a man turns to the Lord the veil is removed" (vv. 15-16). The fact that it is Christ who is instrumental in taking away the veil points both ways. Whose glory is beheld by Christians? The answer can only be that it is the glory of God in Christ. Consequently, when Paul says that "the Lord is the Spirit" he must be referring to God in Christ (cf. II Corinthians 4:6). In any case, the doctrine of the Trinity is clear, that the Father, the Son and the Spirit are one God (see the "Trinitarian" statement at II Corinthians 13:14).

Paul then associates the Spirit of the Lord with the bringing of freedom. In one sense he must be referring to freedom from what he perceived as the trammels of the Jewish law. At another level he seems to interpret freedom as a new openness in the relationship of the believer with the Lord. So, "...with unveiled face beholding the glory of the Lord" all of us, that is those accepting Christ, are being changed. Paul describes this change in beautiful words. It is wonderful to think that we "are being changed into his likeness". This means that the glory we perceive in Christ becomes our glory. We advance progressively into our comprehension of this glory by changing "from one degree of glory to another". This is reminiscent of Paul's mention of the third level of heaven (II Corinthians 12:2). It is as if the pilgrimage into glory goes on beyond this life, that our growth towards God is never-endingly glorious.

Religious people and academics are sometimes accused of living in ivory towers, the implication being that they do not have their feet on the ground of everyday reality. Paul can hardly be accused of living in an airy fairy world without any connection with the world as it is. His practical wisdom is outstanding and the sufferings he underwent are proverbial. Yet, he writes as if perhaps he himself had ascended to "the third heaven". A good parallel lies in the life of Jesus. Our Lord ascended the Mount of Transfiguration to be revealed in glory to the three disciples with him (see Matthew 17:1-13). From that vision of glory Jesus then undertook the way of the cross. Paul understands this duality in life very well. The vision and the hard work go together. Each day for many Christians should surely contain elements of "the glory of the Lord", and that despite being immersed in the day to day concerns of work and the family.

Emily Bronte expressed a similar thought when she wrote:

"No coward soul is mine,
No trembler in the world's storm troubled sphere:
I see Heaven's glories shine,
And faith shines equal, arming me from fear."

(Last Lines)

Bible readings

- II Corinthians 4:3-6 (The light of the gospel of the glory of Christ)
- Romans 8:28-30 (Predestined to be conformed to the image of his Son)

3. Spiritual gifts

Now there are varieties of gifts, but the same Spirit; and there are varieties of service, but the same Lord; and there are varieties of working, but it is the same God who inspires them all in everyone. To each is given the manifestation of the Spirit for the common good.

(I Corinthians 12:4-7)

The gifts of the Spirit are listed at least twice by Paul, at I Corinthians 12:8-10 (just following the above passage) and at Romans 12:6-8. The two lists have very few similarities but a comparison is interesting:

126

Romans	I Corinthians
Prophecy	Prophecy
Service	
Teaching	Utterance of knowledge and wisdom
Exhorting	
Contributing	
Aiding	
Doing acts of mercy	
	Having faith
	Healing
	Working miracles
	Distinguishing spirits
	Speaking in tongues
	Interpreting of tongues

In both cases the gifts are described in Greek as *charismata* (singular *charisma*) which are "gifts of grace". When Paul was compiling these two lists he was presumably "thinking on his feet" rather than giving definitive lists. Indeed, other gifts of grace can be added to these lists. Attempts to classify the gifts from these and other biblical passages (cf. Ephesians 4:7-12; I Peter 4:9-11) have varied, but one useful classification is to divide them into two groups, that is (a) *gifts of communication* (apostleship, prophecy, teaching, speaking in tongues) and (b) *gifts of service* (spreading faith, working miracles, healing, giving alms, helping the needy, organising).

The passage quoted above (I Corinthians 12:4-7) makes a general statement about varieties of gifts, but emphasises that they are all given by the same Spirit. It is the same Lord, the same God who inspires these gifts, and they should be used for "the common good". Paul makes the latter point very graphically in the metaphor of the body of Christ (see vv. 12-26). Towards the end of the discussion he then lists the groups of people who possess these gifts (vv. 27-31). This is all leading up to the great statement about Christian love in Chapter 13. These gifts of the Spirit are wonderful, Paul is saying, but he adds that without love they are of little value.

There has often been argument as to whether the gifts of the Spirit are still extant or whether they ended after the Church had been firmly founded, that is in around the fourth century. Of course the word "charismatic" is often used today to describe a person who is specially gifted. Similarly, the word "Pentecostal" is used (by the members) to describe groups who feel they have the true Spirit of Pentecost. The important question, surely, is whether or not God is still guiding his Church through the Holy Spirit. Most Christians would say that was true. The question next in importance in relation to the point under discussion is whether God gives people special gifts today. The answer in the general sense must surely be affirmative. However, is the Spirit behind such visible phenomena as healing, speaking with tongues and prophesying. Perhaps the answer to this question is a matter of faith. At the same time, it would be unwise to say that none of the gifts of the Spirit is at work in the Church today. From the lists above it is not difficult to identify most of the gifts in today's Church. For example, we have our teachers, our organisers, our contributors, our helpers, and our faith bringers.

Distinguishing between spirits seems to mean deciding what is truly from God and what is not (cf. I Corinthians 2:14). We certainly have to try to do that today, by God's grace. The question is, do some people have a special gift in this direction, apart from commonsense or practical wisdom? Perhaps this is impossible to prove.

Whether or not we have our miracle workers is more difficult to decide, but in any case the miracles recorded in the Bible were produced by God's power working through the agency of people. If miracles happen today, the same will surely apply. For some people there are so many miracles in God's creation that a few more would not be surprising. What can be more miraculous than a newly born baby, or a rose opening, or a rainbow arching, or a wound healing itself? As our Lord himself said: "All things are possible with God" (Mark 10:27).

Bible readings

- Romans 12:3-8 (We, though many, are one body in Christ)
- I Timothy 4:11-16 (Do not neglect the gift you have)

4. Revelation through the Spirit

But, as it is written:
"What no eye has seen, nor ear heard,
nor the heart of man conceived,
what God has prepared for those who love him,"
God has revealed to us through the Spirit.
For the Spirit searches everything, even the depths of God.
                                        (I Corinthians 2:9-10)

These verses express both the mystery and the wonder of the love of God burgeoning within the hearts and minds of those who love him. By no stretch of the human imagination can these spiritual riches be conceived or understood before they are experienced. Even the great rulers of the world have not been able to pierce this secret kingdom of the spirit which had been planned by God before the ages of human history even began (see the preceding verses 6-7). The rulers of Paul's day, that is to say, the Roman authorities, had no inkling of God's purpose, or "they would not have crucified the Lord of glory" (v. 8).

Paul often quotes from the scriptures (i.e. the Old Testament) and from other sources to support his arguments. The text he cites in verse 9, however, is not to be found exactly as it is "quoted". There are similarities with Isaiah 64:4, but some scholars believe Paul is quoting from a work outside the canon of Jewish scripture. There were many such works in circulation and some of them were respected as sacred writings, especially by Jews of the Dispersion who had been brought up outside the traditional homeland.

What is Paul suggesting in the passage quoted above (I Corinthians 2:9-10)? What are the wonders that God has in store "for those who love him"? Paul unpacks this in verses 14-16. The continuity of his argument shows that "the unspiritual man" (literally "the natural or animal part of man") "does not receive the gifts of the Spirit (v. 14). Such things seem very foolish to worldly people. This perspective is still manifestly true today. Many people who are concerned principally with their own pleasures see little of value in religion. As Paul says, they cannot see them because these things "are spiritually discerned" (v. 14).

Christians, on the other hand "have the mind of Christ" (v. 16). This is the treasure store, the source of all love and truth and beauty in our experience. This is "what God has prepared for those who love him." Having made all this clear to his readers at Corinth, Paul then points out that the Corinthians are missing all these wonderful gifts that God has planned for them. His irony is very effective: "But I, brethren, could not address you as spiritual men, but as men of the flesh, as babes in Christ" (3:1) – and they are still not ready, he continues. In other words, they are not behaving as spiritually mature people.

To return to the passage under consideration, Paul says in verse 10: "For the Spirit searches everything, even the depths of God." Paul appears to mean that God and the Spirit are one in thought and action. The parallel with the human mind and spirit is interesting (v. 11), though the precise difference between the mind and spirit is difficult to define. But in relation to God, the implications are that God is in *everything* in some sense because his Spirit "searches everything". Paul is saying that there is no part of heaven and earth which is unsearchable to God. That includes the whole of creation, the whole of space and time, and the inner thoughts of every single human being. To believe that God is totally outside his creation is erroneous. Certainly, he is over and beyond it. In a word, he is transcendent. But he is also within it; that is, he is immanent. At the same time, what has always been implicit (God is in his creation), was made explicit in the Incarnation. As Paul says in another place, "In Christ God was reconciling the world to himself" (II Corinthians 5:19).

For each of us then, as we mature in the faith, God has wonderful gifts. He has already given us uncountable marvels in the universe and in ourselves. Human beings have the capacity to add to these gifts by using the creative powers God has given to them. So not only do we possess all the natural resources and beautiful things in our world, but we also have the many splendoured creations of the poets, artists and composers and others who have special graces from God. However, in addition to all of those things he has given us for starters, he also has the gifts of the Spirit ready for us, as well as the mind of Christ. Elizabeth Barrett Browning was right when she wrote:

"Earth's crammed with heaven,
And every common bush afire with God..."

(Aurora Leigh)

However, that is only the first instalment of many in God's bounty. Paul promises more joys to come, wonders beyond our imagining.

Bible readings

- II Corinthians 1:19-22 (It is God who establishes us)
- Romans 11:33-36 (How unsearchable are his judgements)

5. Receiving the Spirit

Let me ask you only this: Did you receive the Spirit by works of the law, or by hearing with faith? Are you so foolish? Having begun with the Spirit, are you now ending with the flesh? Did you experience so many things in vain? – if it really is in vain. Does he who supplies the Spirit to you and works miracles among you do so by works of the law, or by hearing with faith?

(Galatians 3:2-5)

Paul will not have a return to Jewish legalism at any price. In strong terms he accuses the Galatians of being "foolish" and "bewitched" (the preceding v. 1). He has already reminded his readers that he had previously argued out with Peter (Cephas) the whole question of legalism over against the free grace of God through Christ (2:11). He then asks (in the passage quoted above) how they received the Spirit, whether it was through works of the law or through "hearing with faith". He goes on to contrast the Spirit with "the flesh", which is a double reference to the mark of circumcision in the flesh and to a life ruled by fleshly desires. As often, Paul spares no punches. He repeats the accusation that they are foolish and then drums his message home with a long argument based on the Jewish scriptures (chapters 3-5:12). This is certainly a good strategy, because if Paul is trying to defeat traditional Judaisers he must do so on their chosen battle ground of God's revelation to the Jewish people.

On the question of people "receiving the Spirit", the New Testament suggests various ways in which this comes about. For example, during his resurrection appearances Jesus promised "...you shall be baptised with Holy Spirit" (Acts 1:5). In John's Gospel it is recorded that the risen Jesus "breathed on them", after which he invited them to receive the Holy Spirit (John 20:22). On the day of Pentecost, the Holy Spirit descended unbidden on the gathered disciples (Acts 2:1-4). On some occasions the laying on of hands brought the gift of the Holy Spirit (cf. Acts 8:17; 19:6). On the question of "hearing with faith", this way of receiving the Spirit is described at Acts 10:44. While Peter was speaking, the Holy Spirit fell on "all who heard the word", including Cornelius, the Gentile convert to the faith.

Paul then refers to God "who supplies the Spirit" to them and asks if the miracles brought about by him were achieved by works of the law or by hearing with faith (v. 5). The account of the visit of Paul to Ephesus, where he went shortly after visiting Galatia, includes the following description of miraculous happenings:

"And God did extraordinary miracles by the hands of Paul, so that handkerchiefs or aprons were carried away from his body to the sick, and diseases left them and the evil spirit came out of them" (Acts 19:11-12).

It is fair to assume that this is the sort of miraculous happening that Paul is referring to in his letter to the Galatians. The main point he is making is that it was through faith that these miracles came about, not through the law – just as they received the Spirit by faith and not through works of the law.

It seems that the Galatians were known by Paul to have had deep spiritual experiences. He challenges them: "Did you experience so many things in vain?" (v. 4). What Paul seems to mean is this. If the people are going to turn the clock back to earlier times, when outward customs like circumcision were thought to be necessary and when the Jewish law was paramount, is not the direct operation of the Holy Spirit in vain? Paul feels that the direct relationship between God and the Church, through faith and through the action of the Holy Spirit, has made the law and all it stands for redundant in many respects.

There is a clear parallel for today's Church. Tradition is all very well in its right perspective, but what matters is the personal relationship with God through the day to day action of the Holy Spirit and through the faith of those who pray, not only with their lips, but also deep in their hearts. Laws and customs are useful within the Church, but they are servants to true spirituality, not masters. The Old Testament prophets preached a similar message. Hosea wrote: "For I desire steadfast love and not sacrifice, the knowledge of God, rather than burnt offerings" (Hosea 6:6). In each generation it is necessary to break through the bonds of custom and tradition to a new understanding of the essential truth of God's love. The Holy Spirit cannot be locked in a system or in a church building.

Bible readings

– Romans 7:4-6 (Discharged from the law)
– II Thessalonians 1:11-12 (Every good resolve and work of faith)

6. The Spirit dwells in you

But you are not in the flesh, you are in the Spirit, if in fact the Spirit of God dwells in you. Anyone who does not have the Spirit of Christ does not belong to him. But if Christ is in you, although your bodies are dead because of sin, your spirits are alive because of righteousness. If the Spirit of him who raised Jesus from the dead dwells in you, he who raised Christ Jesus from the dead will give life to your mortal bodies also through his Spirit which dwells in you.

(Romans 8:9-11)

There is undoubtedly a Trinitarian assumption in this passage. The "Spirit of God" is also the "Spirit of Christ". This statement of Paul's also seems to shed light on the old argument between the Eastern and Western Churches. About a thousand years ago the Western Church added a phrase to the earlier creed. This addition had been used unofficially for several centuries before that. Instead of saying only, "...the Holy Spirit... who proceeds from the Father", it was further claimed that the Holy Spirit also proceeded from "the Son". Thus it was that the so called Filioque (and the Son) Clause was added to the creed, now reading, "We believe in the Holy Spirit, the Lord, the giver of life, who proceeds from the Father and the Son."

Once again Paul is contrasting the life of the Spirit with the life of the flesh. In verse 6, just preceding the quoted passage, Paul writes, "To set the mind on the flesh is death, but to set the mind on the Spirit is life and peace." In Paul's view sin and death go together, but "the Spirit of life in Christ Jesus has set me free from the law of sin and death" (v. 2). In our Christian belief, of course, the Holy Spirit is "the giver of life", as noted above. This is not to say that the Father and Son are excluded, because it was the Father who raised the Son from the dead, and it is through Christ that we are raised to life. In any case, the three persons of God are inseparable in action.

Paul assures the Roman congregation, however, that if the Spirit dwells in them, they are not living by the flesh (v. 9). The negative side of this is that if "any one does not have the Spirit of Christ" that person does not belong to Christ. How do people know whether or not the Spirit is dwelling within them? Can we be deceived in this matter? Self deception is always possible, of course, but if a person is trying honestly to live by the Spirit, it seems unlikely that he or she will be completely deaf to the Spirit's voice. A useful criterion by which we can judge ourselves then, according to Paul's thinking, is whether or not we are living in the flesh. If our minds are filled with physical desires and longing for pleasure to the exclusion of all else, then the Spirit has little room to work in us. The truth is that most of us who try to follow Christ are living in the flesh, but aspiring towards life in the Spirit. Paul tells us that this is true of himself when he is aware of his "members at war with one another" (Romans 7:21-25). So Paul was perhaps warning the Romans and ourselves that temptations and dangers are always near at hand. The war between the flesh and the Spirit may be constant in this life.

The translation "righteousness" in verse 10 is misleading. Our spirits are alive, not because of any intrinsic claim to righteousness that we may have, but because of our "justification" by Christ. This is Christ's work in us and not our own moral uprightness. This is clear from the use of the cognate verb in verse 30 of the same chapter:

"And those whom he predestined he also called; and those whom he called he also justified; and those whom he justified he also glorified."

This means that in our spirits, when the Spirit of God in Christ is dwelling in us, we are conforming to the divine will and purpose in thought and action.

If the Spirit of Christ is truly within us, then we are committed to righteous action, with God's help. The inner war of the Spirit should move outwards into the world. The Spirit within us becomes a motive force. With that Spirit in and around us, we may take William Blake's words to heart, though of course, with a universal application:

"I will not cease from Mental Fight,
Nor shall my Sword sleep in my hand,
Till we have built Jerusalem,
In England's green and pleasant land."

(from Milton)

Bible readings

- Ephesians 4:17-24 (Be renewed in the spirit of your minds)
- I Corinthians 1:26-31 (Let him who boasts, boast of the Lord)

7. The Spirit leads us through Christ to the Father

And he (Christ) came and preached peace to you who were
far off and peace to those who were near; for through him
we both have access in one Spirit to the Father.

(Ephesians 2:17-18)

Again Paul puts forward a distinctly Trinitarian view. It
is through Christ that we have access in the Spirit to the
Father. It is as if Christ is our elder brother who is taking us
with him, through the Holy Spirit, to God the Father's
inner sanctuary. In a very real sense we are being formed in
the image of Christ and, therefore, as it says at Genesis
1:27, in the image of God. The initial stage of our creation
is succeeded by another stage in which Christ begins to
refine the first rough shape of our souls. This process
includes access to God through a door opened by Christ,
God's Son, making us all brothers and sisters in Christ.

It is clear from the preceding verses (vv. 11ff.) that
"those who were far off" were the Gentiles, and that "those
who were near" were the Jewish people. Historically there
had been a "dividing wall of hostility" (v. 14) between
Jews and "Gentiles in the flesh, called the uncircumcision"
(v. 11). The Jews themselves had built this dividing wall,
certainly from the time of Ezra onwards, that is probably
from the fifth century BC. Ezra put into action a policy of
isolationism in order to preserve the purity of the Jewish
faith. The Pharisees were the inheritors of that tradition,
and Paul himself had been educated as a Pharisee, so he
would know what he was talking about. The very name
"Pharisees" means the "separated ones". It is clear from the
Gospel stories that the Pharisees regarded Gentiles as virtually untouchable. Even Jesus himself told the twelve
disciples not to go among the Gentiles (Matthew 10:5), but
of course he also healed the daughter of a Gentile woman,
despite having first refused to do so (see Mark 7:24-30).

Paul sees clearly that it was "the blood of Christ" (v.
13) which brought the Gentiles into communion with God.

Christ is "our peace" (v. 14) and he it is who has made all peoples one in himself. When Paul says that Christ "preached peace to those who were far off and peace to those who were near", he means that the word of God in Christ, that is, the gospel, was brought to the Gentiles and to the Jews by missionaries like himself. A more literal translation would be "brought the gospel of peace". Paul refers to God as the "God of peace" in several places (cf. Romans 15:33; 16:20) and Christ is known as the Prince of Peace after Isaiah's prophecy (Isaiah 9:6). Also, of course, Paul's friend and colleague, Luke, saw the birth of Jesus as a reason for the angels to sing, "Glory to God in the highest, and on earth peace among men..." (Luke 2:14).

The Gentiles, including many of the Ephesian congregation, "are no longer strangers and sojourners" but "fellow citizens with the saints and the household of God" (v. 19). It is not clear whether Paul means the saints in heaven or the saints upon earth (the faithful members of the Church). Perhaps he means both. This is true for us. Some of us may have been far from God at an earlier stage in our lives, but when we turn to Christ we, too, are fellow citizens with the saints. Certainly there are some people in today's world who are unfriendly towards the Church and who may also be far from God. The two categories are not necessarily synonymous, of course. However, Christ always offers the possibility of bringing those who are far off into his communion, and hopefully the Church will always be welcoming to newcomers.

The peace which Christ brings through the Spirit refers not only to peace between groups who were formerly at enmity with each other, but also to the inward peace which each of us seeks. The inner life of each person is a smaller version of the war between good and evil which goes on in the wider world. There is "a dividing wall of hostility" within ourselves, a wall between us and Christ. On one side of that wall is the peace and love of God. On the other side is our selfishness and the dislike we have for any interruption in our pursuit of our own ends. The Spirit of Christ within us will remove the dividing wall brick by brick until we are no longer divided within ourselves. The completion of this growth to perfect peace with God and with ourselves may elude us in this life, but it is surely an ideal we should attempt to reach.

Most Christians would try to keep peace within the Christian congregation, but sometimes disagreements do arise. However, if people are open to the Spirit, he will bring peace. The exchange of greetings at the peace during the Eucharist should bring peace to those who are far off from God and from each other.

The ancient words of Aaron's blessing, given to the Aaronic priesthood by Moses, would have been familiar to Paul. It is perhaps helpful for us to ponder on these ancient words and to pray for the peace of God among us and within us:

"The Lord bless you and keep you:
The Lord make his face to shine upon you,
    and be gracious to you:
The Lord lift up his countenance upon you,
    and give you peace" (Numbers 6:24-26).

Bible readings

– Ephesians 4:1-6 ((One body and one Spirit)
– Romans 8:26-27 (The Spirit intercedes for us)

8. We are sanctified by the Spirit

But we are bound to give thanks to God always for you, brethren beloved by the Lord, because God chose you from the beginning to be saved, through sanctification by the Spirit and belief in the truth.

(II Thessalonians 2:13)

This is a very encouraging statement by Paul. The Thessalonians have been unsettled by worries about when the Second Coming of Christ might be due. However, Paul suggests that the prophetic signs of Christ's coming have not yet appeared (2:3-4). This is in contrast to his previous letter when he said that Christ could come at any time "like a thief in the night" (I Thessalonians 5:2). Instead of worrying about the precise date of Christ's arrival, the Thessalonians should be thankful that in such a lawless world they have been chosen by God.

According to Paul their election had been planned by God "from the beginning". This probably refers to God's original plan in creation and not to their own initiation into the Church, though some ancient manuscripts read "as the first converts". The latter is probably an interpretative gloss. In any case, predestination in the personal sense is not necessarily implied. Paul probably intends to say God's eternal plan includes the salvation of the world through Christ.

This salvation is carried out "through sanctification by the Spirit" (or "sanctification of spirit"). The Spirit works within us to bring us to salvation and that process includes "sanctification". The latter is not a word you hear much in the local pub, nor indeed in conversations at the Church bazaar. So what does it actually mean? Has it really something to do with our everyday lives? Or is it just a vague theological word which only applies to the "head in the clouds" type of Christian?

Paul uses a similar expression in his previous letter to the Thessalonians:

"May the God of peace himself sanctify you wholly; and may your spirit and soul and body be kept sound and blameless at the coming of our Lord Jesus Christ."

(I Thessalonians 5:23)

This verse gives us a clue as to what Paul is getting at. Everything we are (spirit, soul and body) and everything we do is dedicated to God. This includes the idea of being separated for God's service. For most Christians this means living in the world, though not according to the world's standards. We should at least attempt to live according to God's standards. This does not mean we have to be "holier than thou" in our attitudes, but it does mean taking seriously the standards we profess when we attend Church.

The literal meaning of "sanctification" is "becoming holy" or perhaps "becoming pure". But we have to remember that we are dealing with a personal God whose holiness is inseparable from his love. He is also a God with his "feet on the ground". You only have to consider the life of our Lord to realise that. This may take us a little nearer to understanding what Paul is getting at. After all, he emphasises love above all other virtues (see I Corinthians 13:13). If God himself is filled with holy love and yet has day to day concerns, possibly that is what we should be aiming for. The Spirit of God is changing us, filling us with his holy love and his concern for the hurt and broken in our world. That is what our sanctification means. If we open ourselves to the creative power of the Holy Spirit he will transform us with both holiness and with love and will make us his instruments in the world.

When Wordsworth wrote his famous sonnet about John Milton he grasped clearly that Milton was both godly and down to earth in his approach:

"Pure as the naked heavens, majestic, free,
So thou didst travel on life's common way,
In cheerful godliness; and yet thy heart
The lowliest duties on herself did lay."

These words could well have been written about St Paul. The great souls who pass through this world seem to have the capacity to practise holiness in the humblest of everyday surroundings.

This does, mean of course, renouncing sin and avoiding deliberate association with evil, but it also means that we

141

befriend people who have got themselves into difficulties of various kinds and that we try to bring them also into a "belief in the truth". The word for "belief" in Greek is the same as the word for "faith". It also includes the senses of "trust" and "confidence". The truth probably refers to the "gospel" mentioned in the next verse (v. 14), together with what that means in relation to Christ as the Son of God. Salvation, then, comes both through the Spirit working in us and also through our belief and faith in God. These are the traditions which Paul taught the Thessalonians and it is in these that they ought to stand fast (v. 15). That advice is good for us today.

Bible readings

- I Thessalonians 5:23-24 (The God of peace sanctify you)
- Acts 26:24-29 (The sober truth)

VIII
Have courage:
God is our help in time of trouble

1. My grace is sufficient for you

And to keep me from being too elated by the abundance of
revelations, a thorn was given me in the flesh, a messenger
of Satan, to harass me, to keep me from being too elated.
Three times I besought the Lord about this, that it should
leave me; but he said to me, "My grace is sufficient for you,
for my power is made perfect in weakness." I will all the
more gladly boast of my weaknesses, that the power of
Christ may rest upon me.

(II Corinthians 12:7-9)

Paul is very frank sometimes. In defending himself as a
true apostle he reports an experience of being "caught up
into Paradise" (v. 3). This is written in the third person but
it is generally thought that Paul is referring to himself.
However, he also points out that God has given him a thorn
in the flesh, "a messenger of Satan", to prevent him from
becoming too elated. What precisely the "thorn in the flesh"
was is uncertain. Epilepsy, recurring blindness, malaria
and stammering have all been suggested. Possibly a serious
form of migraine could have caused the weakness he describes. Certainly migraine can disable people for several
days at a time and its symptoms do resemble a sharp thorn
in the eyes and in the head.

Paul's thrice repeated prayer for relief from his weakness is interesting. He obviously believes that if God
has not positively answered a prayer after three serious

petitions, then the answer must be negative. It means, too, that he felt certain that God was listening. Of course, he has received an answer of a kind in that he has learned to accept his weakness as a spiritual corrective for possible vanity. Moreover, and perhaps more importantly, God has told him a great spiritual truth: "My grace is sufficient for you, for my power is made perfect in weakness." The Greek word for grace (*charis*) is as ambiguous as the English word, but from the context Paul probably means "God's support and help". The word often means "favour", especially referring to the divine favour; and the human response to this as depicted by Paul, is faith.

Of all the spiritual treasures that Paul has bequeathed to us, this experience is one of the most valuable. Many, many people have difficult experiences through illness, imprisonment, bereavement, loss of employment, break up of relationships and a host of other possible tragedies. Yet, God is with us in our weakness. At those times when we are vulnerable God will fill us with his power. The Christ of Calvary will walk with us in the dark times and he will bring us in due course to a resurrection experience.

Paul goes on to say that he is happy to boast of his weaknesses for the very reason that the power of God perfects itself in weakness. Furthermore, in addition to his weaknesses he is content with "insults, hardships, persecutions and calamities" (v. 10). It is at these very times that he is spiritually strong. Of course, Paul is being ironical, even sarcastic. He claims that he has been forced to make these sorts of claims to show that he is not "inferior to these superlative apostles" (v. 11).

In what we sometimes call the "real world" it is power that counts and power usually goes with wealth. Our Lord, however, emptied himself of power, taking the form of a servant, "though he was in the form of God" (Philippians 2:6). Paul, perhaps above all other apostles, understood this and became of no account himself in order to serve the Church. Those of us who try to follow Christ understand that the "real world" is God's Kingdom, and that the world in which we live is a kind of production theatre to enable us to learn from experience. What we learn is to some extent up to us, but God does take a hand, as in the Incarnation. Christ has shown us some of the things we ought to learn and self giving love is at the top of his list. This message is central in the gospels and it is also central in Paul's theology and ethics. The grace of God is also at the very centre of Paul's thinking.

It is not surprising to find that Robert Louis Stevenson, the Victorian poet and novelist, wrote a prayer about God's grace:

> "Give us grace and strength to forbear and to
>   persevere.
> Give us courage and gaiety and the quiet mind,
>   spare us
> to our friends, soften to us our enemies."

It is highly probable that Stevenson was familiar with the writings of St Paul.

Bible readings

– Acts 14:24-28 (Commended to the grace of God)
– Ephesians 3:1-6 (Stewardship of God's grace)

2. He comforts us in all our affliction

Blessed be the God and Father of our Lord Jesus Christ, the Father of mercies and God of all comfort, who comforts us in all our affliction, so that we may be able to comfort those who are in any affliction, with the comfort with which we ourselves are comforted by God. For as we share abundantly in Christ's sufferings, so through Christ we share abundantly in comfort too. If we are afflicted, it is for your comfort and salvation; and if we are comforted, it is for

145

*your comfort, which you experience when you patiently
endure the same sufferings that we suffer. Our hope for you
is unshaken; for we know that as you share in our sufferings,
you will also share in our comfort.*

(II Corinthians 1:3-7)

Paul uses the word "comfort" or related words no less
than ten times in this short passage. It is from this word that
the title Paraclete (Comforter) is derived (also translated
Counsellor or Advocate). John uses the title of Jesus (I
John 2:1) and of the Holy Spirit (John 14:16, 26; 15:26;
16:7). In the passage above Paul says that God the Father is
the one who comforts, but that comfort also comes through
Christ. Indeed, because we share in this comfort, we too
can bring it to others (v. 4). It seems, then, that Paul and
John agree that this capacity to comfort is an important
divine quality, and that like love, it may be borrowed by us.
Certainly, the ability to comfort people in various forms of
distress is a wonderful gift. Although God often comforts
people directly, it seems that he also uses us as his agents in
this respect.

Paul shows that suffering and comfort are complementary to each other. This is not a new idea. The prophet
Second Isaiah said much the same thing, perhaps in more
dire circumstances:

> "Comfort, comfort my people,
> says your God.
> peak tenderly to Jerusalem,
> and cry to her
> that her warfare is ended..." (Isaiah 40:1-2).

The prophet was announcing that God would bring his
suffering people back to Jerusalem from their exile in
Babylon. In Paul's case perhaps a more general statement
is intended, that in times of persecution or hardship, God's
comfort in the form of his love and grace are freely available to those who turn to him.

Paul is undoubtedly speaking from personal experience. His sufferings for Christ's sake are well known, and he gives an account of them in the Corinthian letter(s) (see II Corinthians 6:3-10; 11:21-29). Accordingly, when he challenges the Corinthians to "patiently endure the same sufferings that we suffer" (v. 6 above), they would know what he was talking about. They would probably realise that their own sufferings were not all that great compared with Paul's. At the same time the quality of "patient endurance" is valuable in any adversity, and if that is combined with comfort from God, then the experience may be seen to have positive elements. The man or woman who is physically handicapped and in constant pain may not have been specifically in Paul's mind, but anyone in that situation will certainly appreciate what Paul is saying. Some people amazingly rise above such sufferings and by God's grace seem to attain a measure of serenity through their "patient endurance". This is not to say that suffering in itself is good, but it is a fact that life does bring people to various forms of suffering. But then, our Lord himself suffered terribly and this shows that God is prepared to share in human suffering.

It is perhaps reasonable to suppose that Paul sometimes said psalms and prayers to himself or for his companions when he was journeying. Possibly at times the prospect in front of him seemed daunting. As he clambered, staff in hand, through some rocky valley not too far from Corinth he might well have said:

"Even though I walk through the valley of the
    shadow of death,
I fear no evil;
for thou art with me;
thy rod and thy staff,
they comfort me" (Psalm 23:4).

Bible readings

- II Thessalonians 2:16-17 (God's eternal comfort)
- Romans 1:9-12 (Encouraged by each other's faith)

3. The peace of God which passes all understanding

Rejoice in the Lord always; again I will say, Rejoice. Let all men know your forbearance. The Lord is at hand. Have no anxiety about anything, but in everything by prayer and supplication with thanksgiving let your requests be made known to God. And the peace of God, which passes all understanding, will keep your hearts and your minds in Jesus Christ.

(Philippians 4:4-7)

After mentioning certain members of the congregation by name, encouraging them to show team spirit (vv. 2-3), Paul gives some unforgettable general words of encouragement. He packs tightly into half a dozen lines a number of invaluable pieces of advice. First, he invites the congregation to rejoice. He emphasises his point be repeating the phrase (v. 4). They should rejoice at all times, because the Lord is with them and they are in the Lord. When Paul says, "The Lord is at hand", he probably means, as verse 4 suggests, that God is always there, waiting to show his favour. He goes on to say that they should have no anxiety about anything. This is very much in the spirit of the advice of Jesus in the Sermon on the Mount (Matthew 6:25-34). At the same time, some argue that Paul is referring to the imminence of Christ's coming when he says, "The Lord is at hand." This may also be true. In Paul's mind the reality of God in Christ was so tangible, that while the reappearance of Christ before the whole world would serve to convince others of God's presence, Paul was already so deeply involved in a personal relationship with the Lord, that the change for him would simply be a change of focus.

Paul also advises that the people of the Philippian Church should, "Let all men know your forbearance" (v. 5). This probably refers to the idea of working together without quarrelling (see v. 3). We all know how difficult this can be, especially if people of strong character and unshakeable convictions are working together. It is too easy for people to cut across someone else's viewpoint or "territory" and for arguments, even feuds, to develop. Paul is suggesting that a measure of "forbearance", that is resisting the temptation to flare up, will be for the common good.

It is obvious that Paul sees as central to the Christian life a pattern of prayer and worship (v. 6). This is not to be separated from other aspects of life. Paul recommends that "*in everything*, by prayer and supplication with thanksgiving" they should let their requests be made known to God. The Greek word for "thanksgiving" here is *eucharistia*, and Paul uses the equivalent verb to describe the institution of the Eucharistic sacrament (cf. I Corinthians 11:24). Consequently, it seems more than possible that Paul had the sacrament in mind in giving this advice.

If the people follow Paul's advice they will experience a deep, inner peace, "the peace of God, which passes all understanding" (v. 7). Some of the psalmists knew of this kind of quietness in the soul. In Psalm 17, for example, the psalmist says:

"Keep me as the apple of the eye;
hide me in the shadow of thy wings..." (Psalm 17:8).

Similarly, the writer of Psalm 46 writes:

"Be still and know that I am God" (Psalm 46:10).

It is not always easy to find the peace Paul talks about. The top of the mind is usually filled with so many worldly concerns, that it is difficult to feel God's peace all the time. But Paul may be referring to a deeper level of peace, a peace that is undergirding everything we do, however busy we may be. At certain times of the day, if we follow Paul's advice and follow a serious prayer life, we may return to this deep pool of peace that by God's grace may lie within us. Of course, there are times when we may be deeply disturbed about something, an injustice a friend has experienced or the serious illness of a dear friend. Even these difficult times may be faced with deep equanimity if we have God's peace within us. It is God's gift, but the depth of our faith and commitment may open the way for God to give us this kind of peace.

The poet Dante gives us a possible clue as to the way in which we may find God's peace:

"And in His will is our peace" (Paradiso iii 85)
[E'n la sua volontate è nostra pace].

If we are truly seeking to find God's will in our lives, and if we are seeking to ally our wills with God's will, then the peace of God may descend upon us.

Bible readings

– I Thessalonians 5:12-22 (The will of God in Christ Jesus for you)
– Ephesians 6:18-20 (Pray at all times in the Spirit)

4. God did not give us a spirit of timidity

Hence I remind you to rekindle the gift of God that is within you through the laying on of my hands; for God did not give us a spirit of timidity but a spirit of power and love and self control.

(II Timothy 1:6-7)

Here Paul is speaking directly to his friend Timothy. He reminds his "beloved child" of the gift he received "through the laying on of my hands" (v. 7, but see I Timothy 4:14). This custom of the laying on of hands has survived, according to the Church, without a break from the time of the apostles to the present time. Paul himself was sent on his missions after the laying on of hands (Acts 13:3). In Old Testament times the imposition of hands was seen as a form of blessing (Genesis 48:8-14). Joshua was given the spirit of wisdom "for Moses had laid his hands on him" (Deuteronomy 34:9). The Levitical priests were ordained through the laying on of hands by the people (Numbers 8:10-11). In the New Testament the receiving of the Spirit and baptism were sometimes associated with the laying on of hands (Acts 8:14-19; 19:5-6). The first deacons had the hands of the apostles laid upon them (Acts 6:5-6). It seems, then, that when Paul laid hands upon Timothy, he felt he was acting as God's agent in confirming Timothy's ministry.

Paul is asking Timothy to "rekindle the gift of God" he had originally received through the laying on of hands. Paul does not specify what the gift of God Timothy received was, but it is fair to conclude from what follows that Paul is referring to Timothy's gift of preaching and teaching. For example, Paul writes: "...preach the word, be urgent in season and out of season, convince, rebuke, and exhort, be unfailing in patience and teaching" (II Timothy 4:2). Any Christian can get into a rut and may need a timely reminder of the enthusiasm and the fire that he or she displayed at an earlier time. Paul's pastoral care is very good in that respect. He often reminds his readers that they need to live up to their vocations (see, for example Ephesians 4:1; Galatians 5:1; II Corinthians 13:1-3).

Timothy, and indeed all of us, ought not to be timid when it comes to witnessing to the faith, by word or deed. The spirit we have been given is one "of power and love and self control" (v. 7). Whatever our position in the Church, if we have committed ourselves in the Spirit to the Christian life, then our lives should be open to the power of God. People can deliberately shut themselves off from God's power. God has given all of us that option. However, most committed Christians would not consciously wish to do that. In the main, the call to serve God is genuinely accepted, but not always carried through with every fibre of our being. Not many of us can live with the absolute commitment of St Paul, but each of us can do much more than we imagine, if we let God use the gifts we have been given.

People who have had the disadvantage of being born rich (cf. (Matthew 19:24) or the disadvantage of being born poor; people from all walks of life throughout the Christian centuries, have shown that God miraculously changes people, if they allow his power into their lives. Choose a saint at random from any book of saints and you will find an ordinary human being with the same weaknesses that we have. Yet, God has so worked in and through that person, that something wonderful has been achieved. St Peter and St Paul, for example, are portrayed in the Bible as having very human weaknesses, and yet God chose each of them to do great things.

Along with God's power comes his love. Love is also a great miracle worker. People don't need to be clever or wise in order to love others. The capacity to love may be a greater gift than any other. Paul certainly thought it was all important (see I Corinthians 13). To express Paul's thought in a slightly different way: if you are a great artist, or a great writer, or a great musician, or a great politician, or a great archbishop – all of these are of little value without love. Take the example of a man and his wife who foster forty children over a period of years and give them the love and care they need. In God's eyes, those two people may be of greater stature than any monarch or prime minister. God's ways are not our ways and he searches everyone to the root of the soul.

Along with God's power and the love that should go with it, Paul suggests we should also cultivate self control. We can achieve little unless we have the discipline to harness our abilities, whatever they may be. Even love is less valuable if it is out of control. The great advantage of the Christian vocation is that it offers a way of life which is subject to the disciplines of prayer and worship. Those who "do their own thing" without reference to the Church community and what it offers, may well make useful achievements, but if their powers were properly harnessed they could achieve so much more. It was Archimedes who said that if he had a long enough lever and somewhere to stand he could move the world. God has such a lever. Its axis is the cross. What he moves is not the planet, but the world of thought and action in which people play out their lives. He is moving the world and he is using us to do it. It is his power in us and his love in us that will bring about the kingdom. However, nothing worthwhile was ever achieved without hard work and discipline. That is Paul's message to Timothy and to us.

Bible readings

– Acts 13:1-3 (Set apart for me Barnabas and Saul)
– II Corinthians 13:5-10 (Hold to your faith)

5. Share in suffering as a good soldier of Christ Jesus

Share in suffering as a good soldier of Christ Jesus. No soldier on service gets entangled in civilian pursuits, since his aim is to satisfy the one who enlisted him. An athlete is not crowned unless he competes according to the rules. It is the hard-working farmer who ought to have the first share of the crops. Think over what I say, for the Lord will grant you understanding in everything.

(II Timothy 2:3-7)

Practical as always, Paul uses three human occupations to illustrate his message. First he points to the soldier, then to the athlete, and finally to the farmer. Not only has a soldier to accept his share of suffering, but he has to be

153

single-minded. He cannot allow himself to be involved too much in civilian affairs when he is on service. His responsibility is to the one who has enlisted him. In a similar way, the Christian on active service is responsible to God, the one who called him (or her). He must not allow himself to be distracted from the work to which he has committed himself. There are several hymns on the theme of soldiering in the Christian sense. Perhaps the best known is the one by Sabine Baring-Gould:

> "Onward Christian soldiers,
> Marching as to war,
> With the cross of Jesus
> Going on before."

Also, of course, some Christian groups have based their ideals on the parallel of soldiering. The Salvation Army is a good example. In this sense, Paul's words have borne much fruit.

Similarly, the athlete has to keep to certain rules. If he breaks the rules and wins by cheating, he will not receive the laurel crown usually awarded to the winner. To extend this parallel a little further, it is of no use the footballer playing his game according to the rules of cricket. The Christian likewise has to live and work by given rules. Towards the end of the chapter, Paul describes what the Lord's servant ought to be like:

> "And the Lord's servant must not be quarrelsome but kindly to everyone, an apt teacher, forbearing, correcting his opponents with gentleness."
>
> (II Timothy 2:24-25)

In addition to those duties, of course, there are the basic Christian rules about love and loyalty to one's calling. The Christian who does not try to live up to these ideals will not be crowned by Christ at the end of his earthly life.

The analogy of the farmer, too, is very expressive. The

farmer who does not work hard will not produce good crops. Even if he is working for somebody else, he is entitled to the first share of the produce. In the same way, a Christian who does not follow his calling diligently will not achieve good results. The teacher or the preacher will not bring in a harvest of converts. Another equally valid interpretation is to see the seeds of faith growing in the soul, as in the parable of the sower (see Mark 4:1-20). If the Christian does not work on the word of God within him (or her), then the plants may not produce any fruit at all. However, by God's grace, hard work in the faith will allow the seed of God's word to produce a person growing towards Christ in holiness and love.

After encouraging Timothy ("my son" in v. 1) to further endeavours, Paul then writes, "Think over what I say, for the Lord will grant you understanding in everything" (v. 7). Paul presumably means that Timothy will gain a deeper understanding of the faith and of the way to run a church. Such understanding cannot come about outside the context of prayer. If anyone is to "understand everything", that is, gain a true perspective on the things that truly matter in life, and if God is to help him to full understanding, then the prayer relationship is critical. If all aspects of life are dedicated to God, of course, there is a sense in which everything we think or do is a prayer. There is an old proverb which says, "To work is to pray." Also, if we give serious and regular thought to what we are about in God's service, this in itself is a form of prayer. If we think deeply about our vocations, perhaps God will help us also to a fuller understanding.

Bible readings

- Philippians 2:25-30 (A fellow soldier)
- I Corinthians 9:24-27 (Run that you may obtain the prize)

6. Put on the whole armour of God

Finally, be strong in the Lord and in the strength of his might. Put on the whole armour of God, that you may be able to stand against the wiles of the devil. For we are not contending against flesh and blood, but against the principalities, against the powers, against the world rulers of this present darkness, against the spiritual hosts of wickedness in the heavenly places. Therefore take the whole armour of God, that you may be able to withstand in the evil day, and having done all, to stand. Stand, therefore, having girded your loins with truth, and having put on the breastplate of righteousness, and having shod your feet with the equipment of the gospel of peace; besides all these, taking the shield of faith, with which you can quench all the flaming darts of the evil one. And take the helmet of salvation, and the sword of the Spirit, which is the word of God.

(Ephesians 6:10-17)

Most writers are influenced either directly or indirectly by the works of previous authors. This influence may sometimes be perceived in the style or in the imagery or in the content. In the above passage there seems to be little doubt that Paul is either deliberately imitating, or has been influenced by, the work of the so called Second Isaiah. For example, Isaiah writes:

"He put on righteousness as a breastplate,
and a helmet of salvation upon his head;
he put on garments of vengeance for clothing,
and wrapped himself in fury as a mantle."

(Isaiah 59:17)

The writer of the Book of Wisdom also uses similar imagery, and doubtless Paul would be familiar with that work, which was probably written in the first century BC (see Wisdom 5:17-21).

The difference in Paul's use of the imagery is that he

156

transfers the dress for battle from the person of God to the person of the individual Christian. This is the mark of Paul's genius and inspiration. He does not blindly follow the writers who have influenced him, but with a deft twist and turn uses the imagery in a new way. He uses similar imagery in the Second Letter to the Thessalonians (cf. 5:8).

What Paul does, in fact, is to take a range of the great Christian principles and to arrange them in an extended metaphor to show that these principles will protect us against temptation and against evil powers. If the principles are simply listed as truth, righteousness, the gospel of peace, faith and salvation, then the poetry is lost; but Paul does not choose to write a boring catalogue of theological ideas – instead he composes one of the most evocative and powerful pieces of writing in Christian literature.

Part of the effect Paul achieves is given by the background of a cosmic battle between the powers of good and evil. This is not a unique idea. The Book of Revelation describes Armageddon in lurid terms (Revelation 16:14-16); and from the Qumran community come writings of a similar nature in the War Rule, which describes the war between the sons of light and the sons of darkness. The opposition of light and darkness appears also in John's Gospel (see John 1:5). Indeed, the opposition of light and darkness is prefigured in the creation story (Genesis 1:1-4). There may well be deliberate apocalyptic references in Paul's description, especially in v. 12. Certainly, in some of his letters he seems to expect the imminent second coming of Christ (I Thessalonians 4:13-18). However, the main thrust of Paul's description is to help Christians in their everyday struggles against evil. Yet, it is important to remember that each individual struggle is part of the greater, cosmic war against evil powers.

There are many situations in life when this passage from Ephesians may be helpful to the individual. Even in the workplace, Christians are sometimes attacked for their beliefs. Ridicule and sarcasm are used to try to persuade the Christian to shift his position. Paul's advice in such a situation is really helpful. He says that when we have done all, then we have to stand fast (v. 13). Flexibility is all very well in some situations, but when it comes to basic principles we may have to be unbending in our views.

Many of us at some time in our lives are tempted to do something we know to be wrong. It may be that we see somebody needing help but for some reason it would be embarrassing or dangerous to act. It may be that breaking our marriage vows or vows of celibacy is the temptation. It may be that something that doesn't belong to us is temptingly easy to take. It may be that telling a lie is going to avoid awkward consequences, but at the same time get somebody else into trouble. There are legions of temptations to lead us all astray, but the defence is clear. "Therefore take the whole armour of God..."

As we gain experience we become more aware of our strengths and weaknesses. If we know have an "Achilles' heel", that is one area where we need to be especially vigilant. As the First Letter of Peter says:

"Be sober, be watchful. Your adversary the devil prowls around like a roaring lion, seeking someone to devour. Resist him, firm in your faith..." (I Peter 5:8).

Bible readings

– Colossians 1:11-14 (He has delivered us from the dominion of darkness)
– I Timothy 6:11-16 (Fight the good fight of the faith)

7. Stand firm in one spirit

Only let your manner of life be worthy of the gospel of Christ, so that whether I come and see you or am absent, I may hear of you that you stand firm in one spirit, with one mind striving side by side for the faith of the gospel, and not frightened in anything by your opponents. This is a clear omen to them of their destruction, but of your salvation, and that from God.

(Philippians 1:27-28)

In this passage Paul puts an emphasis on the strength of Christian community. If the people of God are standing firm "in one spirit" and are "with one mind striving side by side for the faith of the gospel", then they need not be frightened of any opponents. In standing together, however, it is vital that they live in a manner "worthy of the gospel of Christ". Paul describes what manner of life this ought to be at the beginning of the next chapter (2:1-4). The congregation ought to be "of the same mind" and to have "the same love" (v. 2). The bonds of the spirit which should bind the community are then strong enough to stand against the attacks of people who live by the standards of the world.

Paul believes that those who oppose God will be destroyed. On the other hand, those who have a living faith in Christ are destined for salvation by God himself. Of course, in day to day life there are many complexities. Paul paints a black and white picture which is very effective in putting over his message. However, there are many shades of grey among Christians as well as among non-Christians. Not every Christian lives up to the ideals of the faith. Many non-Christians try to lead good lives. At the same time, there are those who deliberately flout the word of God, and possibly those are the people Paul is saying are doomed for destruction.

The personal influence of Paul on the churches he has founded or helped to found is very strong. The very fact that the Church has accepted his letters into the canon of the New Testament speaks for itself. In promoting that influence, Paul's policy of keeping hold of the reins is very apparent here. He writes "...let your manner of life be worthy of the Gospel of Christ... whether I come and see you or am absent" (v. 27). Paul was obviously something of a dynamo and his personality must have been a powerful one, despite his admissions of weakness (cf. II Corinthians 12:8-10) – but such admissions are characteristic of his absolute honesty and integrity. When we meet someone like that, especially in the context of the Church, we wonder where the inner power comes from. Paul himself is quite clear that he is Spirit filled and that it is the power of God working through him that enables him to overcome whatever obstacles are put in his way (cf. Philippians 1:19-20). His biography in Acts of the Apostles records a tale of almost superhuman endurance (see, for example, Acts 14:19-20; 16:22-24; 28:3-5).

So much of Paul's advice is relevant in modern times. For example, if he spoke today in a market square about the community and the body of Christ, he would almost certainly emphasise the principle of standing "firm in one spirit". We might wonder what he would make of the one hundred and one sects and denominations which are to be found in many towns. Perhaps he would preach a "back to basics policy", a policy of faith and love, in which all the fragments could be pieced together again. At the same time, he would almost certainly condemn much of what he would see in the world around us. A world in which a pop singer is paid more than a prime minister would possibly inspire him to write a strong letter to the Church in Rome or in Canterbury or in Capetown. On the other hand he might well have something to say about politicians and their standards of judgement, especially in relation to the Third World. The fact is that Paul's letters and the Bible as a whole have a message for every generation. The Church needs to interpret that message in language the world can understand.

Bible readings

– Ephesians 4:1-7 (Unity of the Spirit in the bond of peace)
– I Thessalonians 5:5-11 (Build one another up)

IX
Living by faith

1. He who through faith is righteous shall live

*For I am not ashamed of the gospel: it is the power of God
for salvation to everyone who has faith, to the Jew first and
also to the Greek. For in it the righteousness of God is
revealed through faith for faith; as it is written, "He who
through faith is righteous shall live."*

(Romans 1:16-17)

Paul writes in the previous verse (v. 15) that he is "eager
to preach the gospel" to the Christian community in Rome.
We know from Acts of the Apostles that he did eventually
reach Rome and that he was able to preach there for at least
two years (see Acts 28:30-31). The author of Acts (probably Paul's friend Luke the physician) actually reports that
Paul preached "the kingdom of God", a phrase which Paul
does use sometimes in his letters (see for example Romans
14:17; I Corinthians 4:20). However, the expression "the
righteousness of God", mentioned above (v. 17) as being
revealed in the gospel, is also often used by Paul and seems
almost to have a similar meaning to the phrase "kingdom
of God".

It may seem a little odd to us that Paul should feel the
need to say, "For I am not ashamed of the gospel...",
because it is quite obvious from our perspective that it was
absolutely central to his life. At the same time, some of us
may feel the need to make the same sort of statement if we
are in the company of people who scoff at religious belief.
We may wish to make explicit that we are proud of the
gospel whatever other people may think. In Paul's day also

there would be no shortage of sceptics, so perhaps Paul is intending to encourage the Romans not to be ashamed of their religious faith. Rather should they be faithful and open in their confession that Jesus Christ is Lord (cf. Romans 1:4-6).

Paul claims that the gospel brings "salvation to *everyone* who has faith", though he does also make the point that this opportunity comes "to the Jew first and also to the Greek". By allowing this precedence to the Jew, Paul probably means simply that the Jews were chosen initially by God and so, because Jesus was also a Jew, they were given the first opportunity to accept the gospel. However, Paul makes it clear later in the letter that in Christ both Greek and Jew have equality (Romans 10:12). He is using "Greek" in a general sense to refer to non-Jews. Greek was the lingua franca of much of the area where Paul travelled on his missions and Greek civilisation had been spread several centuries earlier by the conquests of Alexander the Great.

Through the gospel, God's righteousness is "revealed through faith for faith" (v. 17). This could be more literally translated "out of faith into faith". The difficulty with the word "faith" is that it has a range of meanings, not only in English, but also in Greek and Hebrew, the languages of the Bible. The word Paul uses can also mean "belief, trust or confidence" or even a "pledge of faithfulness". Another difficulty in interpreting this key text is whether the word "faith" refers to God's "faithfulness" or to human "faith" or "faithfulness". The phrase "through faith for faith" may mean that the whole process of revelation is a question of human faith from beginning to end; or it could mean that through God's "faithfulness" to his promises, human "faith" is encouraged. In either case, it is clear that the virtue of faith is an important one for us to acquire, taking in the whole range of possible meanings of the word.

When Paul quotes from the scriptures at the end of verse 17, he is citing a text from the prophet Habakkuk 2:4 which reads:

162

"Behold, he whose soul is not upright in him shall fail, but the righteous shall live by his faith."

(N.B. the RSV gives "faithfulness" as a possible alternative for the last word in the quotation.)

The question is, did the prophet mean *God's (his) faithfulness* or did he mean *man's (his) faith*? Paul omits the word "his", but the Greek translation of the Old Testament accepts that Habakkuk intended to refer to God's faithfulness, changing the word his into my to make this clear. It is probable that Paul sometimes quoted the scriptures from memory, so he may have omitted the word "his" by accident. On the other hand he could have left it out deliberately. He may even have left it purposely ambiguous. This would mean that God's faithfulness and human faith are both required in the process of salvation. This would be supported by the previous phrase "through faith for faith". It should also be remembered that God's grace is operating in the situation where human faith encounters the living Christ.

Martin Luther was greatly exercised in trying to understand Paul's letter to the Romans, especially these verses (1:16-17). At first he believed God's righteousness should be interpreted mainly in terms of punishing the unrighteous. Later, he was led to emphasise justification by faith through God's grace, and he felt that he had been led into a new life. The righteousness of God, he concluded, was a cause for love rather than fear. A balanced interpretation would still take the idea of God's wrath very seriously, but Paul invariably turns to God's mercy and love for salvation. In that respect, Luther was right. However sinful we feel, if we repent and pray for God's help, it will surely come. Paul also writes: "My grace is sufficient for you, for my power is made perfect in weakness" (II Corinthians 12:9).

- Romans 3:21-26 (Justified by his grace)
- Galatians 3:10-14 (The promise of the Spirit through faith)

2. Fight the good fight of the faith

But as for you, man of God, shun all this; aim at righteousness, godliness, faith, love, steadfastness, gentleness. Fight the good fight of the faith; take hold of the eternal life to which you were called when you made the good confession in the presence of many witnesses.

(I Timothy 6:11-12)

Paul is using a very traditional form of address to Timothy in calling him "man of God" (cf. Deuteronomy 33:1; I Kings 12:22). Characteristically, Paul is exhorting his friend to shun sin and to embrace the Christian virtues, listed here as righteousness, godliness, faith, love, steadfastness and gentleness. The idea of being gentle seems to be contradicted by the following challenge to "fight the good fight of the faith". However, Paul is presumably referring to the fight against temptation. In fact, the Greek word used for "fight" provides the derivation for the English word "agonise" (cf. the word "conflict" at Philippians 1:29-30). The message for us is perhaps one we already know: the Christian life is not easy.

To make the "good confession" can mean to make a promise or to consent to something. In this case it appears that Timothy has earlier made a confession of faith, that is, he has promised to hold to his faith. Christ himself, according to Paul, "made the good confession" before Pontius Pilate (v. 13). This must surely mean that our Lord held to his commitment to remain faithful to his vocation as the suffering servant of God, despite the daunting prospect of a painful death. Whether Timothy made his confession at his baptism or at the outset of his work as a Christian leader is not clear. He may have been baptised as a child (cf. II Timothy 3:15). However, he seems also to have made a commitment involving circumcision (cf. Acts 16:3).

As noted in the previous section, the Greek word for "faith" has a range of meanings, one of which is a promise of fidelity. When a Christian opens his or her life to Christ in faith, not only is he placing his trust in a person and acknowledging a set of beliefs, he is also undertaking to hold to the ideals to which he has committed himself, usually before witnesses. Even to stand with a group of other Christians to recite the creed is to make a commitment to what the creed states. However, assent to a creed can never be the main thrust of faith. The reality of Christ and faith in his commitment to us is what we are involved in. Nevertheless, it is helpful to remember that our faith does involve belief in a set of propositions which are derived ultimately from the Bible.

In a similar way, to "fight the good fight of the faith" involves standing for what we believe as well as holding to our personal trust in God. We may have to defend the faith in a variety of circumstances. Sometimes we may be challenged as to the reality of God himself. At other times we may be challenged to defend a belief in one aspect of our faith, the resurrection, for example. Yet again, we may be challenged to stand by the ethical principles which go with being a Christian. A discipline of prayer and worship are part of the armour which will defend us, as well as the armour of faith and the other Christian virtues (see especially Ephesians 6:10-20).

Perhaps the greatest gift that faith brings is "eternal life" (v.12). It is interesting that Paul invites us to "take hold" of this wonderful gift. Later in the chapter Paul repeats the invitation, though phrased slightly differently. He writes, "...take hold of the life which is life indeed" (6:19). The Greek expression translated "life indeed" is not easy to interpret. Literally it would be "the life which really exists." In verse 12 that same life is described as "eternal", which means "without beginning and without end". God's being, of course, is of that nature, and in some sense, when we grasp eternal life we are becoming aware that we are part of God's being in the here and now. At the same time, the resurrection life must surely have been in Paul's mind. The "life eternal" seems to resemble the kingdom of God in that it is both present and in our future expectations (cf. Mark 1:15; Luke 17:21).

The awareness of God's being within us as well as around us is one of the most wonderful gifts that faith brings. This is akin to "breathing the Spirit". Just as we breathe air into our lungs each moment of life, so we breathe the Spirit of God into our souls. When we know this deep within ourselves our quality of life is changed. We are then living the life eternal of God's kingdom.

Bible readings

- II Corinthians 4:16-18 (The things that are unseen are eternal)
- Romans 10:10-13 (No one who believes in him will be put to shame)

3. The armour of faith

But since we belong to the day, let us be sober, and put on the breastplate of faith and love, and for a helmet the hope of salvation. For God has not destined us for wrath, but to obtain salvation through our Lord Jesus Christ, who died for us so that whether we wake or sleep we might live with him.

(I Thessalonians 5:8-10)

The great triad of Christian virtues, faith, love and hope (cf. I Corinthians 13:13), are placed by Paul within one of his favourite metaphors, that is, the image of God's armour

166

(cf. Ephesians 6:10-20). Faith and love together form a breastplate which will guard us against the powers of Satan; and our hope of salvation is a helmet to protect us from those depths of despair into which we are liable to fall without God's help. Certainly, some human situations seem hopeless. For example, if a young person is told he or she is dying of cancer and that there is no cure, life must seem very grim indeed. However, our Lord himself plumbed the depths of human misery in his passion, and out of that chasm of apparent hopelessness he brought hope for all of us, whatever our situation.

It is interesting that Paul groups together faith, hope and love and then stands them over against God's wrath. To be sure he takes God's wrath very seriously (cf. Romans 1:18; 2:5), but in his theological discussions he invariably comes back to God's love and, of course, he believes that love is the greatest human virtue (cf. I Corinthians 13:13). However, human love is derived from God's love. It is a gift in our first creation, but through Christ it is an even more abundant gift in a further stage of our creation. This is where faith takes its stand beside love. It is through faith in Christ that we have access to God's love and grace.

Faith is not to be taken frivolously. Paul recommends a sober approach to our religion and in this he is surely right. While a sense of humour is always helpful in keeping our sense of proportion and while, no doubt, God himself must laugh in his own way because after all he created laughter, nevertheless, sobriety is necessary when it comes to our serious commitment to the faith. Paul's metaphor in the preceding verses (vv. 4-8) contrasts darkness with light and sleep with keeping awake. Christians need to be vigilant and wakeful because "we belong to the day". The metaphors are a little confusing because of the earlier reference to the day of the Lord coming "like a thief in the night" (v. 2). Nevertheless, the point is made that serious commitment requires serious thought. Our faith is our lifeline to God and through it we have the opportunity of salvation through Christ.

167

In the day to day passage of events there are many darts which try to pierce the armour of our faith and love. Sometimes we fall to minor temptations and are able to pick ourselves up again. However, a host of minor temptations may be just as deadly as one of those major sins which assail us perhaps once in a lifetime. Evil is insidious as well as being scandalously bold. Our Lord expresses this very well in his teaching when he says:

> "When a strong man, fully armed, guards his own palace, his goods are in peace; but when one stronger than he assails him and overcomes him, he takes away his armour in which he trusted, and divides his spoil."
>
> (Luke 11:21-22)

We need to look to our armour, to mend it and to polish it. We should embark upon each day with our armour unpierced, or at least repaired from any darts that struck us during the previous day. Faith and love express themselves best when undergirded by a spiritual discipline. This is not to condemn the inspiration of the moment which may often lead to new insights or loving deeds. However, we are less likely to fall into temptation if we approach each day soberly, putting on "the breastplate of faith and love", as Paul suggests. E.H. Blakeney expresses this thought very well in a verse of his well known hymn:

> "Strong in the power of faith,
> From doubt and care set free,
> We tread the appointed path
> That brings us home to thee."

Bible readings

- Romans 2:5-11 (He will render to every man according to his works)
- Ephesians 6:10-13 (Be strong in the Lord)

168

4. Saved by God's grace

For by grace you have been saved through faith; and this is not your own doing, it is the gift of God – not because of works, lest any man should boast. For we are his workmanship, created in Christ Jesus for good works, which God prepared beforehand, that we should walk in them.

(Ephesians 2:8-10)

Paul makes explicit here that it is God's grace which saves us, but that faith is the power line which enables God's grace to work within us to bring about our "conversion" to holiness. Faith in itself is not what saves us. As Paul clearly says, "...this is not your own doing." However, faith is an essential element in the process and God offers this gift freely for us to accept it or to reject it. Paul is aware that some have turned their backs on a faith they once had. He writes to Timothy, for example, "For the love of money is the root of all evils; it is through this craving that some have *wandered away from the faith* and pierced their hearts with many pangs" (I Timothy 6:10). Fortunately, the invitation to return to the faith is always open (cf. II Corinthians 7:9-10).

Paul continues his thought by saying that the saving process comes about "not because of works", but then immediately points out that good works are expected! We are "created in Christ Jesus for good works", he insists. The difficulty in interpreting Paul and other parts of the Bible is that sometimes interpreters make a banner of a particular phrase and then take it out of context. This has sometimes happened in relation to faith and its part in salvation. If Paul's thoughts are taken as a whole it is clear that he does not see faith as an excuse for not doing good works. Moreover, faith is only one of a number of factors which characterise our relationship with God. God's grace, for example, meets our gift of faith and expands into a love that completes us and fulfils us. As Julian of Norwich put it:

"In his love he clothes us, enfolds us and embraces us; that tender love completely surrounds us, never to leave us" (Revelations of Divine Love).

Any one element in the process of salvation cannot be separated from the others.

Our characters (or souls) are "his workmanship created in Christ Jesus for good works" (v. 10). This is stating the process of salvation in another way: it is an act of creation by God in Christ. As said previously, our faith is an ingredient in the continuing creation of our personalities, but it is our Lord himself who is transforming us. The prophet Jeremiah compares God to a potter:

"Then the word of the Lord came to me: 'O house of Israel, can I not do with you as this potter has done? says the Lord. Behold, like the clay in the potter's hand, so you are in my hand, O house of Israel.'"

(Jeremiah 18:5-6)

Paul is taking a similar view here. We are God's workmanship. Paul, in fact, uses the same metaphor as Jeremiah in his letter to the Romans (cf. 9:19-24). In the Romans passage he argues that God will "make known the riches of his glory for the vessels of mercy, which he has prepared beforehand for glory, even us whom he has called" (19:23). This idea that God has planned our development beforehand is repeated in the passage under discussion (Ephesians 2:8-10). However, Paul is emphasising the good works that should go along with our new life in Christ.

While reading passages such as this, perhaps we should examine ourselves sometimes to see whether we are cooperating with the divine plan for ourselves. How far is each of us involved in doing the work of Christ in the supermarket and in the office, in the factory and in the pub? No doubt we feel we are involved in Church life, but is our church life extending into the life of the general community? Our Lord himself pronounced his judgement upon the matter:

"Let your light so shine before men, that they may see your good works and give glory to your Father who is in heaven" (Matthew 5:16).

It is faith in Christ which opens our spirits to let him shine within us. When he shines within us he shines through us into the world.

Bible readings

– Colossians 3:17 (Do everything in the name of the Lord Jesus)
– Ephesians 4:7-16 (The work of ministry)

5. Stand firm in the faith

Be watchful, stand firm in your faith, be courageous, be strong. Let all that you do be done in love.
(I Corinthians 16:13-14)

Paul's advice in these verses is slotted between comments about practical arrangements and commendation of those who have served the gospel well. It may be that Paul had earlier decided to end the letter with this comment and then later had further thoughts. In any case, it serves to illustrate that he never lost an opportunity to exhort his readers to aspire to the highest standards in their religion, both in practical giving and in acquiring a firm faith.

Yet again Paul stands faith and love together, almost as a summary of what is essential in following Christ. It is well known that Paul placed love as the greatest virtue of all (cf. I Corinthians 13:13) so if pressed to define his priorities in this respect he would probably say, "Love and have faith!" At the same time he would probably add that the two are inseparable in true religion. Those who have faith in Christ and allow him into their hearts will

171

inevitably learn love. Those who love in the Christian sense have already allowed Christ into their hearts and their faith will surely grow.

Paul is well aware that occasions for back sliding and opportunities to fall into the snares of temptation are manifold. Hence he advises his readers to be watchful. He probably means that people should be watchful of themselves, though he does sometimes warn congregations against particular people who might lead them astray (see I Corinthians 5:1-8). This advice to be watchful is good for us also. Self criticism is no bad thing provided it does not become neurotic. A good spring clean of our attitudes and actions now and again is wise. For each of us there may be a besetting sin that needs a bit of severe self pruning, whether it be laziness or covetousness or constant grumbling or whatever. Just as a house and a garden need care and attention, so do our spiritual lives.

The advice "to stand firm in your faith" is also relevant to all Christians, as in Paul's day, so in ours. There is a tendency to emphasise the personal relationship with God and, of course, this is a necessary element in true faith. However, asserting the truths of the faith along with our fellow believers can also help us to be firm in our belief. To stand together in worship, repeating the creed, retelling our faith in song and hymn, listening to and interpreting the word of God, and above all receiving communion together, all of these firm up our individual faith in God. It was the poet George Pope Morris who wrote in another context, "United we stand, divided we fall" (The Flag of our Union). These words are surely true for the Church.

Paul also advises us to be courageous and strong. This is not always easy, especially if we happen to be shy or timid by nature. Yet, certain Christians have achieved great deeds, despite their natural frailty. Take Bernadette Soubirous, for example, a simple country girl who was uneducated and suffered from poor health. Her faith and courage undoubtedly changed the face of the Christian Church. Or take Gladys Aylward, a lady of small stature, who against all obstacles and difficulties went to work as a missionary in China. Her courage and determination came from her faith in Christ.

Paul then says, "Let all that you do be done in love." This is certainly not sentimental in its intention. It can be extremely difficult to act in love (*agapē*) in some situations. It is even hard within the Christian congregation always to act in love. Unhappily, jealousies and rivalries appear even there. Yet, no one would deny that Paul is right. We are all conscious of having fallen short of the Christian ideal from time to time, but we usually know what we ought to have done. We know we ought not to have repeated that piece of salacious gossip; we know that we shouldn't have shouted angrily at Mrs So and So (even if she is a so and so); we know that we shouldn't have told a fib about not being available to help at a function; and so on. Nevertheless, if we did not have the ideal of love, we should probably behave much more badly than we do at the moment. And, of course, we know that we can repent and try to make amends, provided our obstinacy can be overcome. It was Matthew Arnold who wrote:

"The pursuit of perfection, then, is the pursuit of sweetness and light... He who works for sweetness and light united, works to make his reason and the will of God prevail" (Culture and Anarchy).

As Christians we are at least pursuing perfection, even if we rarely attain it. With the help of Christ, in prayer and action, and our reason supporting our faith, we ought always to strive to bring our ideals into reality.

Bible readings

- II Corinthians 13:5-10 (Examine yourselves)
- Philippians 1:27-30 (Stand firm in one spirit)

6. We walk by faith, not by sight

So we are always of good courage; we know that while we are at home in the body we are away from the Lord, for we walk by faith, not by sight.

(II Corinthians 5:6-7)

In an almost Platonic way Paul speaks of the body as the temporary home of the eternal soul. However, Paul is always "concrete" in his imagery. In that respect, the translation conceals an important verbal pattern in the Greek which actually contrasts being *at home* in the body with being *away from the home* of Christ. The implication is that our true home is in heaven with Christ. In fact, Paul starts the section by comparing the body to an "earthly tent" (5:1). This would be very apt for him as he was by trade a tentmaker (see Acts 18:3). Furthermore, he would know that the tabernacle or tent used by the Israelites in the wilderness was the early pattern for God's dwelling upon earth, later the temple (see Exodus 25:8-9; Psalm 132:1-5). (It is worth noting that in John 1:14 a literal translation would be: "And the Word became flesh and pitched his tent among us...") Consequently, it is quite possible that Paul had in mind the idea of a pilgrimage in which our tents are temporary dwellings as we travel through the wilderness of this life.

In the preceding verse 2 Paul suggests that in this life "we groan, and long to put on our heavenly dwelling". Then after a complicated mixed metaphor he says that God has prepared a permanent home for us and "has given us the Spirit as a guarantee" (v. 5). This prepares the way for the mysterious statement that "we walk by faith, and not by sight" (vv. 6-7). The Spirit moves mysteriously and invisibly among us. Our Lord himself explained how we can see the results of the Spirit's action, though we cannot see where the Spirit goes or whence it comes (John 3:8). Not only does God move in a mysterious way, but our destination on our pilgrimage is also mysterious. We cannot see

174

our heavenly home, though we have a pattern for it in the earthly Jerusalem (cf. Galatians 4:25-26). Therefore, as we march on our earthly pilgrimage we need to have faith in the things we cannot see. This inevitably reminds us of the words of Jesus to Thomas the doubter:

"Jesus said to him, 'Have you believed because you have seen me? Blessed are those who have not seen me and yet believe'" (John 20:29).

Of course, there are certain helpful things we are able to see. We have the Church and the Scriptures, both of which connect us in a very real way with our Lord of the Incarnation. The Church is the guardian of the faith and the Scriptures help us to define our faith. Yet again, we have the whole of creation to examine with all of our senses and, as Thomas Aquinas found when he was seeking proofs of God's existence, the universe gives its own testimony. As the psalmist puts it:

"The heavens are telling the glory of God;
and the firmament proclaims his handiwork."

(Psalm 19:1)

We have our reason, we have our dreams, we have our hopes. To the mind that is even half aware, God speaks very clearly.

So God has not left us without some guidelines. Nevertheless, God himself is invisible and the dimension of heaven, with all its saints and angels, is also invisible. It is not surprising, therefore, that some people find great difficulty in accepting any such reality beyond this life. That is what Paul is referring to when he talks of walking "by faith and not by sight". To those who are in the darkness of doubt, Paul's own writings and the witnessing of the other Biblical writers make an inviting gateway to the path of faith. Trial by prayer can also be a helpful beginning. Through the first stumbling prayer the Holy Spirit will find a way to help us to faith. As Tennyson writes: "More things are wrought by prayer / Than this world dreams of" (The Passing of Arthur).

There is a wonderful echo of Paul's comment on "walking by faith and not by sight" in the Letter to the Hebrews:

"Now faith is the assurance of things hoped for, the conviction of things not seen" (Hebrews 11:1).

Paul believed firmly in the life to come. It would be wonderful for each one of us to be able to say with him:

"I have fought the good fight, I have finished the race, I have kept the faith" (II Timothy 4:7).

Bible readings

- Acts 22:12-16 (Paul receives his sight)
- Ephesians 5:1-14 (Walk as children of light)

7. Faith in the Son of God

I have been crucified with Christ; it is no longer I who live, but Christ who lives in me; and the life I now live in the flesh I live by faith in the Son of God, who loved me and gave himself for me.

(Galatians 1:20)

In the section of which this verse is a part Paul is arguing for an openness to Christ's grace through faith and an abandonment of the idea that the Jewish law can ever save people from the effects of their sins. To the Galatians he gives an account of the great dispute he had with Peter in Jerusalem over this very matter (vv. 11-16 preceding). His argument then turns to the crucifixion and resurrection as they work within us (cf. Romans 6:3-11).

176

Paul takes the idea of the death of his old self to the point that he claims it is Christ who lives within him, and not himself. This must be a hyperbole to emphasise his point, of course, because he is still Paul of Tarsus. However, his meaning is very clear. His inner life has been colonised and transformed by Christ. This process is not yet complete, nor is it without pain and struggle (cf. Romans 7:15; 8:26).

The means by which these changes are taking place is the faith he has in "the Son of God". This a very explicit statement of who Christ is (cf. Romans 1:4). It is interesting that Paul is recorded in Acts of the Apostles as having preached an important sermon at Antioch, which was on the borders of Galatia. In the course of that sermon he says:

"And we bring you the good news that what God promised to the fathers, this he has fulfilled to us their children by raising Jesus; as also it is written in the second psalm, 'Thou art my Son, today I have begotten thee'."

(Acts 13:32-33)

It is quite likely that Paul preached a similar sermon to the congregation addressed in the letter. This sermon shows one of the grounds for Paul's faith that Jesus Christ is Son of God. The resurrection for Paul was God's great sign to the world, the confirmation that Jesus of Nazareth was his Son. Paul obviously takes the psalm, which was originally a royal psalm about the kings of Israel, to be a prophecy about Christ.

Paul's experience at his conversion on the Damascus road would naturally be the starting point for his faith in Christ and the fulcrum for his transformation into a new person. No doubt the testimony of Stephen and other Christians would have planted the first seeds of the faith within Paul. Paul was confronted by the living Christ and this experience changed the course of his life. Similar experiences, though not necessarily so dramatic, have changed the lives of many other people since then and often Paul himself has been the instrument of bringing people to Christ through his own testimony. The list of saints in the Church's calendar is a list of men and women who have found "faith in the Son of God".

Paul's experience of Christ was one of love. It was Paul above all other New Testament writers who worked out in detail a theory of Christ's atonement. He states in the verse under discussion that "the Son of God, who loved me gave himself for me". Those few words summarise the meaning and purpose of our Lord's Passion. Elsewhere in his letters Paul explains the atonement more explicitly (cf. Romans 3:21-26). The point of his argument is that if the law could justify people, "then Christ died to no purpose" (Galatians 1:21).

The experience of Christ that Paul had is freely available to all of us. To turn to the Son of God in faith, and to accept his love, is to accept a wind of change that will sweep through the whole of our lives. Sometimes this will be like a whirlwind. At other times it will be a gentle breeze. But the wind (or Spirit) of God will not let us stand still. We are invited to set out on the ocean of faith and seek God's will. If we do that we shall have some wonderful and unexpected experiences.

Bible readings

- Romans 6:3-11 (Alive to God in Christ Jesus)
- Galatians 1:11-17 (Set apart before I was born)

8. The word of faith for salvation

The word is near you, on your lips and in your heart (that is, the word of faith which we preach); because, if you confess with your lips that Jesus is Lord and believe in your heart that God raised him from the dead, you will be saved.
(Romans 10:8-9)

God's word is not far away from us. We may speak it or we may store it in our hearts. Paul seems to have in mind a text in Deuteronomy:

"But the word is very near to you; it is in your mouth and in your heart, so that you can do it."
(Deuteronomy 30:14)

Of course, in the context of Deuteronomy it is God's law which is the word (Deuteronomy 30:16). We have to remember, though, that certain key texts in Deuteronomy which were worn on the wrist, on the forehead, or fastened to door posts, included the Shema:

"Hear, O Israel: The Lord our God is one Lord; and you shall love the Lord your God with all your heart, and with all your soul, and with all your might. And these words I command you this day shall be upon your heart..." (Deuteronomy 6:4-6).

This is a key text in Christianity also. However, in the text under discussion (Romans 10:8-9) Paul is describing the "word of faith" which is related to Christ, who actually was and is God's love in action.

To confess this word of faith by saying "Jesus is Lord" (cf. I Corinthians 12:3) is to make a commitment to Christ. That commitment, however, needs to be in the heart also. Possibly Paul had in mind the new covenant described by Jeremiah:

"I will put my law within them, and I will write it upon their hearts; and I will be their God and they shall be my people" (Jeremiah 31:33).

However, Paul would no doubt substitute "word of faith" for "law". This indicates that Paul's concept of God's word has taken on a new meaning, though he does not actually define Christ as "the Word" as John does (cf. John 1:1). At

179

the same time, Paul's association of God's word with the living Christ is so close that it cannot be said that he differs radically from John's Gospel on that point (Colossians 3:16).

Paul sees preaching as the means by which the word of faith is sown (cf. the Parable of the Sower, Mark 4:1-20). When this word is spoken by the listener and received in the heart, then he or she is justified and saved (Romans 10:10). Reading "the word of faith" may be just as effective as preaching it. Paul would probably have expected that his letters would be read to congregations and of course millions of people have read his letters right up to the present day. The number of people who have been converted to Christianity by reading "the word of faith" as expressed by Paul must be very great indeed.

We can only give thanks to God for Paul's work as apostle and missionary. St Peter Damien expressed this well:

"From heaven's height Christ spake to call
The Gentiles' great apostle, Paul,
Whose doctrine, like the thunder, sounds
To the wide world's remotest bounds."

(Translated by J. M. Neale)

Bible readings

– II Timothy 1:8-14 (Testifying to our Lord)
– Ephesians 1:11-14 (The gospel of your salvation)

IX

The Christian community

1. One Lord, one faith

I therefore, a prisoner for the Lord, beg you to lead a life worthy of the calling to which you have been called, with all lowliness and meekness, with patience, forbearing one another in love, eager to maintain the unity of the Spirit in the bond of peace. There is one body and one Spirit, just as you were called to the one hope that belongs to your call, one Lord, one faith, one baptism, one God and Father of us all, who is above all and through all and in all. But grace was given to each of us according to the measure of Christ's gift.

(Ephesians 4:1-7)

Paul was "a prisoner for the Lord" in at least two senses. Historically he was put in prison several times for his beliefs (see for example Acts 16:23; 22:24). However, he was also a prisoner for the Lord in a metaphorical sense, because he was in conscience bound for life to his vocation in Christ. At any rate, possibly writing from a Roman prison and probably with deliberate ambiguity, Paul authenticates his appeal for unity in the Church by citing this evidence of his own deep commitment to the faith.

The call to be a Christian is a call to follow Christ's way of humility and service. Paul invites his readers to behave with "all lowliness and meekness, with patience, forbearing one another in love" (v. 2). In this way it will be possible to "maintain the unity of the Spirit in the bond of peace" (v. 3). Very similar is Paul's thought in Galatians 5:22: "But the fruit of the Spirit is love, joy, peace, patience, kindness, goodness, faithfulness, gentleness, self-control...". This is good advice for any Christian congregation. It is also good advice for the Church as a whole, advice which has often been ignored. In that respect it is unfortunate that historically members of the Church have had many bitter quarrels which have led to the formation of breakaway groups. The result of such past disagreements is the fractured Church of modern times. To produce "the unity of the Spirit in the bond of peace" in the universal Church will need much prayer and much patience. Unity of the Spirit, of course, does not necessarily mean that every congregation has to be cloned to an exact pattern. However, unity of purpose and unity with God's will are worthy goals for the Church as a whole as well as for local congregations.

Just as the Spirit is one, so is the body of Christ one (v. 4). In Greek, as in English, the word for body may refer to the physical body and also by extension to a group of people united by a common bond. Paul uses the word frequently to refer to the spiritual body of Christ (cf. Romans 12:5; I Corinthians 10:16; Colossians 1:18). Paul is emphasising the importance of the "oneness" of the Church as Christ's body as opposed to those who are "tossed to and fro and carried about with every wind of doctrine" (v. 14). He extends his thought by pointing out that Christians share the same hope, the same faith in the same Lord, and the same baptism (v. 4). This sharing should be true in relation to Christian groups today, but in the less than ideal world in which we live, there is often disagreement about the way baptism should be administered, for example. The question is, does the Holy Spirit differentiate between different baptismal customs? We do not know the answer to that question for certain, but the train of Paul's thought seems to indicate that there is only one baptism.

Paul goes on to say, by way of a climax, that there is after all only one God and that he has fathered all of us (vv. 5-6). Everything that exists is subject to his authority because he is "above all and through all and in all" (v. 6). Paul would certainly have approved of the sentiment expressed by John Greenleaf Whittier in his well known hymn:

"Dear Lord and Father of mankind,
Forgive our foolish ways!
Re-clothe us in our rightful mind,
In purer lives thy service find,
In deeper reverence praise."

Yet Paul always turns to the grace of God as expressed through Christ. This too was given "to each of us according to the measure of Christ's gift" (v. 7). Paul does not say that some received more or less grace than others. The grace of Christ is free (i.e. a gift) and it is universal (cf. Romans 3:21-26), which again highlights the equality of all human beings before God. It is true, of course, that in certain respects some human beings have been given more special gifts than others, but such gifts carry special responsibilities. However, God's grace in the spiritual sense is like a vast fountain through which anyone who is thirsty may be satisfied.

Paul himself lived by God's grace and he was very conscious of the fact that he was in need of it, especially in his less exalted moments:

"...but he said to me, 'My grace is sufficient for you, for my power is made perfect in weakness.'"

(II Corinthians 12:9)

The Church in its weakness also depends on God's grace, and the Spirit who is one is always at work among us. The unity of which Paul writes may come unexpectedly nearer to reality sooner than we think. God is full of surprises.

Bible readings

- Romans 12:3-8 (Though we are many, we are one body)
- I Corinthians 12:12-13 (All baptised into one body)

2. Christ is the head of the body

He is the head of the body, the church; he is the beginning, the first born from the dead, that in everything he might be pre-eminent. For in him all the fullness of God was pleased to dwell, and through him to reconcile to himself all things, whether on earth or in heaven, making peace by the blood of his cross.

(Colossians 1:18-20)

After describing Christ's part in creation (preceding verses 15-17), Paul goes on to say that Christ "is the head of the body, the church". This is more than a statement that Christ is the leader of the Church, though obviously that meaning is included. To be sure, this in itself is a statement full of deep meaning, because it involves a belief in the risen Christ who is now actively engaged in leading his Church. Also within Paul's statement lies the metaphor of the head and the body, a parallel with the physical body in which the brain is the controlling factor. Paul surely has in mind also the images used elsewhere of the members of the body all having a part to play in the functioning of the whole. Christ is clearly that part of the body which is in ultimate control of all the other parts (see I Corinthians 12:12-31). Underlying this imagery, of course, is the sacrament of the Eucharist in which Christ's body is shared by the faithful in a wonderful way and through which they are bound together in fellowship.

This Eucharist is the outward and visible sign of Christ's presence in the Church and in the world. There is continuity within the Church from the moment that Christ gave thanks and blessed the bread and the wine, declaring them to be his body and blood (I Corinthians 11:23-26), right up to the present time. It is this re-enactment of Christ's sacrifice on the cross that reminds us constantly that "he is the first born from the dead" (v. 18).

Through this continuing tradition of the Eucharist Christ's work of reconciliation is presented to the Christian community as a living reality. "God was pleased... through him to reconcile to himself all things, whether in earth or in heaven, making peace by the blood of his cross" (v. 20). Because the Church is the body of Christ it is the Church which ought to be the agent of reconciliation within the world and the supreme peace maker. In order to pursue this vocation the Church needs to be reconciled within itself, to be at peace within itself. The Church which is divided and quarrelling is not living up to its vocation in this respect.

Paul is also making a great Christological statement when he asserts that "in him (Christ) all the fullness of God was pleased to dwell" (v. 19). A parallel thought is expressed at II Corinthians 5:19 where Paul writes, "...in Christ God was reconciling the world to himself." The Greek word translated "fullness" implies not only that God was fully in Christ, but also that in Christ God fulfilled his will in the world (cf. Romans 13:10).

If then, Christ is head of the body, the Church, and if God is in Christ, then the Christian body is called to do God's work in the world. Where there is misunderstanding either within or outside the Church, Christians ought to try to bring the light of understanding; where there is conflict either within or outside the Church, Christians should strive to bring peace; where there is ignorance of God's love (hopefully not within the Church) Christians have the responsibility of demonstrating that love, not in a theoretical way, but by actively giving love. A few Christians over the centuries have managed to get it right. St Francis was such a one and his writings reflect his real Christly love:

"Lord, make me an instrument of thy peace.
Where there is hatred let me sow love;
Where there is injury, pardon;
Where there is doubt, faith;
Where there is despair, hope;
Where there is darkness, light;
Where there is sadness, joy."

Bible readings

– Ephesians 1:15-23 (Christ is head over all things)
– II Timothy 2: 20-26 (The Lord's servant)

3. The household of God

So then you are no longer strangers and sojourners, but you are fellow citizens with the saints and members of the household of God, built upon the foundation of the apostles and prophets, Christ Jesus himself being the cornerstone, in whom the whole structure is joined together and grows into a holy temple in the Lord; in whom you also are built into it for a dwelling place of God in the Spirit.

(Ephesians 2:19-22)

Paul is particularly addressing Gentiles (Greeks) in calling his readers former strangers and sojourners. In Israel the sojourner was a non-Israelite who had chosen to live with the Jews. Sojourners had legal rights such as freedom from oppression and permission to pick up the harvest leftovers. Nevertheless, they were not of God's people. In the new Israel of the Christian Church, however, the former strangers and soujorners have equal rights with Christian Jews (cf. v. 15).

In order to demonstrate this new equality, Paul uses another of his brilliant extended metaphors to describe the relationship of the Church and its members in Christ. The

Church is described as the household of God. "Household" is a more personal word than that for a building. Nevertheless the metaphor of the building is drawn upon to make Christ's position in the Church clearer. Both the word for "household" and the word for "house" are cognate with the word *oikoumenē* (the inhabited world) from which the word ecumenical is derived.

The cornerstone of a building is, of course, vital in holding the structure together. Paul would know well that there was a corner stone theology in the Old Testament. Psalm 118:22, for example, reads:

"The stone which the builders rejected
has become the head of the corner."

Originally this was about the psalmist who, after being rejected, was apparently later exalted. Jesus took this passage to refer to himself (e.g. Matthew 21:42).

Another important "cornerstone" passage is at Isaiah 28:16 which reads:

"Behold I am laying in Zion for a foundation
a stone, a tested stone,
a precious cornerstone, of a sure foundation..."

This refers to the stonework of the temple but is symbolic for God's presence with the people of Israel. Paul refers to this passage at Romans 9:33 to describe Christ as a stone to stumble over for unbelievers, but as a strong refuge for the believer. All this is implicit in the reference to the cornerstone in the passage under discussion (Ephesians 2:19-22).

Christ, then, is the corner stone of the household of faith but both prophets and apostles have had their part in erecting the building. The whole structure is God's dwelling place, as the Jewish temple was formerly believed to be. At the same time each Christian who is part of the new structure is also a dwelling place for the Holy Spirit. The metaphor is almost stretched beyond its limits when Paul

187

talks of the building "growing" into a holy temple. Nevertheless, the meaning is clear. The Church is a growing and living society.

The passage is helpful at a very practical level. Any strangers who enter the Church as converts are on equal terms with longer standing members. All Christians are made aware that each of us is an important part of the building, but that Christ is the keystone without which the building would collapse. Further, the Church is growing and changing. It does not remain the same, though the foundations are unchanging, just as God is essentially unchanging while yet allowing change to happen within and around himself. The words of J. Chandler inevitably come to mind:

> "Christ is our cornerstone,
> On him alone we build;
> With his true saints alone
> The courts of heaven are filled:
> On his great love
> Our hopes we place
> Of present grace
> And joys above."

Bible readings

–   I Corinthians 3:16-17 (You are God's temple)
–   II Corinthians 5:1-10 (A house not made with hands)

4. All one in Christ

For as many of you as were baptized into Christ have put on Christ. There is neither Jew nor Greek, there is neither slave nor free, there is neither male nor female; for you are all one in Christ Jesus. And if you are Christ's, then you are Abraham's offspring, heirs according to promise.

(Galatians 3:27-29)

This short passage is the climax of a section (chapter 3) in which Paul emphasises God's promise made to Abraham as prior to God's law as given to Moses. Paul's purpose is to show that through God's promise all are equal before God and that those who insist that the law must be kept to achieve salvation have misunderstood God's intention.

The importance of baptism in Paul's mind is clear. To be baptised is to have put on Christ just as one puts on clothing. To be "clothed with Christ" is a very expressive metaphor. Clothes or, of course, armour (cf. Ephesians 6:11), are protective and to have the protection of Christ is a wonderful experience. In Paul's own case baptism indicated a complete change in his way of life which penetrated his very soul (cf. Acts 9:19).

To have "put on Christ" is to have become a new person. At the same time baptism is an introduction into the Christian family. Within such a family there can be no differentiation between various categories of people. The person who was previously an orthodox Jew has the same status as the person who was previously a pagan Greek. The rich freeman has the same status before God as his own slave, though this does not release the slave from his earthly bondage (see the Letter to Philemon). In God's presence men and women are of equal value. All are "one in Christ Jesus," claims Paul.

As part of his argument Paul shows that all Christians, whether or not they are of Jewish origin, are descendants of Abraham. This is a vital point, because Paul sees God's revelation to Abraham as part of a progressive revelation which was to lead to the Incarnation. Naturally, the Jewish people would feel that Abraham was their forefather and that other nations were not of the chosen people. Paul, however, insists that the concept of God's chosen people has become universal. The promise to Abraham, though given within a Jewish context, does state that by Abraham "all the families of the earth shall bless themselves" (see Genesis 12:1-3). It is interesting in this connection that Muslims also regard Abraham as their spiritual forebear.

The implications of Paul's argument for the Church today are fairly obvious. There should be no racial barriers. A person's sex does not make any difference to that person's opportunity of receiving God's grace. Only with regard to the legitimacy of slavery would we take issue with Paul, but even so, he insists that before Christ slaves are equal to those who are free. It would be foolish, of course, to argue that a Russian is exactly the same as a Brazilian, or that a man is exactly the same as a woman. They are clearly different in many respects. However, that is not the point of the argument, which is that God's promise is for all, regardless of race or sex. That promise includes the gift of God's grace and incorporates the love of Christ. Whatever our human situation, God is with us.

Bible readings

– Colossians 3:12-17 (Perfect harmony)
– Romans 10:11-13 (The same Lord is Lord of all)

5. One bread and one body

The cup of blessing which we bless, is it not a participation in the blood of Christ? The bread which we break, is it not a participation in the body of Christ? Because there is one bread, we who are many are one body, for we all partake of the one bread.

(I Corinthians 10:16-17)

Paul places a great emphasis on the importance of the Eucharist. This passage is complementary to his description of the founding tradition of the Eucharist which he gives later in the same letter (I Corinthians 11:23-26). Perhaps the most interesting word is "participation" which does not do full justice to the original Greek word (*koinonia*), though it does provide an important nuance. The Greek

190

word in question also means "fellowship" or "communion". Paul uses it elsewhere of the "fellowship" of the Holy Spirit (cf. Corinthians 13:13). The word is also used in Acts of the Apostles in association with the breaking of bread (see Acts 2:42).

The idea of communion means a sharing of fellowship with God and also with others receiving the sacrament. There is a parallel with Jewish communion sacrifices which Paul draws out (v. 18). Of course, the old sacrificial system was made redundant by the sacrifice of Christ and Paul is fully aware of that. Nevertheless, he is prepared to draw the parallel for the sake of Jewish readers in particular.

At the same time, in the preceding verses 1-5, Paul points out that the ancient Hebrews in their wilderness wanderings partook of supernatural food and drink (see Exodus 16:4, 35; 17:6). He does not miss the opportunity to point out that the Rock from which the Israelites drank was Christ (v. 4). This is one of the clearest statements by Paul that Christ was pre-existent and that he was and is eternally within the Godhead.

Paul also makes the point, for the benefit of Gentile converts in particular, that to eat food and to drink wine previously sacrificed to idols is offensive. Indeed, he says, "You cannot drink the cup of the Lord and the cup of demons. You cannot partake of the table of the Lord and the table of demons" (v. 21). In effect, the worship of Christ replaces both Jewish and pagan worship, and at the heart of the worship of Christ is the Eucharist.

To drink from the communion cup is to drink of the blood of Christ: to eat the sacred bread is to share in the body of Christ. Christ is the only bread, the one true bread, and those who partake of the one bread are one body. The pun on the word "body" is deliberate because Paul knows that the sacred bread is the body of Christ and that the Church is also the body of Christ. This is true both in microcosm and in macrocosm. When the members of a small congregation receive the elements together they are one in Christ and they are the body of Christ in that place. Further, when any part of the Church receives the Eucharist, the members are at one with God and at one with the whole Church of God, not only on earth, but also in heaven.

The unity of the body of Christ transcends the disunity of the Church as we perceive it. Christ is with all who take part in the Eucharist despite differences of interpretation and differences of practice. This is the true reality and the Church needs to find a way to reflect Christ's unity of body in its outward expression. Diversity of practice would not necessarily be an untrue reflection of the unity of the body of Christ, but at the moment we have disunity alongside diversity. It is difficult to see how this can be God's will for the Church. In any case, in an uncertain and changing world it is well to remember the proverb, "United we stand, divided we fall." It is true that Jesus told Peter that the "powers of death" would never prevail against the Church (Matthew 16:18), and no Christian can doubt that that is ultimately the case. Yet, in particular times and places groups of Christians do fall away and it would be a great strength to the whole Church if we took Paul's words seriously: "We who are many are one body, for we all partake of the one bread..." (v. 17).

Bible readings

- I Corinthians 5:6-8 (The bread of sincerity and truth)
- I Corinthians 1:4-9 (Called into the fellowship of Christ)

6. The Christian proclamation

For I received from the Lord what I also delivered to you, that the Lord Jesus on the night when he was betrayed took bread, and when he had given thanks, he broke it, and said, "This is my body which is for you. Do this in remembrance of me." In the same way, also the cup, after supper, saying,

192

"This cup is the new covenant in my blood. Do this, as often as you drink it, in remembrance of me." For as often as you eat this bread and drink the cup, you proclaim the Lord's death until he comes.

(I Corinthians 11:23-26)

Paul is reminding the Corinthians of the true meaning of the Eucharistic meal. It seems that some of the congregation have been partying, rather than taking part in the sacrament of Christ. At the same time others have gone hungry (see preceding verses 20-21). In that context he reminds them of the tradition of the Eucharist that he himself received "from the Lord". Paul certainly wasn't present at the original Last Supper, and there is no record of a special revelation about this matter from our Lord himself to Paul. While not ruling out the possibility of such a revelation, it seems likely that Paul is also saying that the Church's tradition was from Christ himself and that this is the tradition he is recommending to his readers.

This description of the Eucharist is the earliest known written instruction about the sacrament. The Gospels are generally assumed to have been written later than Paul's letter. There are slight variations between what the various accounts in the Gospels say and what Paul says. That is to be expected because local traditions would almost certainly vary. For example, Luke is the only Gospel which agrees with Paul in its invitation to repeat the sacrament "in remembrance of me" (Luke 22:19). However, it is well known that Luke was Paul's companion on various missions, so it is not surprising that such agreement occurs.

These central words of the Eucharist are so familiar to us that it is sometimes tempting to believe that we fully understand them. However, there is a great mystery enshrined in the sacrament which goes beyond the words and even goes beyond the elements of bread and wine in any particular presentation of the sacrament. It is also true that there are different interpretations of what the words and the sacrament actually mean. Some parts of the Church emphasise the sacrificial aspect of the Eucharist while others emphasise the sacrament as a memorial. There is also dis-agreement about exactly how Christ is present in the sacred elements. Perhaps for most of us it is sufficient to believe that Christ is truly within the sharing of his body and blood without trying to pierce the God-with-us mystery of the sacrament. Those who feel they have explained the mystery have probably merely scratched the surface. It would be as easy to explain the Virgin Birth or the Resurrection as it would be to explain the meaning of the sacrament, which means, in effect, that we are confronting the inexplicable miracles of the divine action in the world.

At the same time there are aspects of the Eucharist which are interesting to ponder. For example, it is a fact that Jesus pronounced the words recorded by Paul and others before the crucifixion and resurrection. Our Lord was aware that his actions and words at the Last Supper with his disciples would be perpetuated and that he would be the living Christ of the bread and the wine. One result of this Christly presence in the communion or mass is that there is a direct bond between God and the Church. This not only binds together each participant with Christ, but it also binds together the whole body of Christ upon earth, that is the Church. It is sometimes said that Jesus did not found the Church. From a limited human perspective this may be true, but the deeper truth is that Christ consciously founded the community of his body and blood at the Last Supper.

Paul also says that as often as we "eat this bread and drink this cup" we proclaim the Lord's death until he comes (v. 26). It is generally thought that Paul and his contemporaries expected the imminent return of Christ into the world. As we know, this did not happen. However, Paul's words about the Second Coming are not invalidated because his immediate expectation did not materialise. Indeed, it is part of Christian belief that Christ will come again. This thought is enshrined in the Christian creeds.

It is not surprising that many beautiful hymns have been written about the sacrament of the Eucharist. To quote just part of one such hymn may remind us of the beauty and spiritual depth which we encounter at the altar or communion table. The original of this hymn was written in the seventh century and the translation is by J.M. Neale.

"Draw nigh and take the body of the Lord,
And drink the Holy Blood for you outpoured.

"Saved by the Body and the holy Blood,
With souls refreshed we render thanks to God.

"Salvation's giver, Christ the only Son,
By his dear Cross and Blood the victory won.

"Offered was he for greatest and for least,
Himself the Victim, and himself the priest."

Bible readings

– Jeremiah 31:31-34 (The new covenant)
– Luke 22:7-23 (The last Supper)

7. Walking in newness of life

Do you not know that all of us who have been baptized into Christ Jesus were baptized into his death? We were buried therefore with him by baptism into death, so that as Christ was raised from the dead by the glory of the Father, we too might walk in newness of life.

(Romans 6:3-4)

In this part of his letter to Rome Paul is engaged in a complicated argument about law and grace. However, in case his readers believe that they are free to continue in sin

195

so that God's "grace may abound" (preceding verse 1), he emphasises that their baptism signified the death of sin for them. Paul's interpretation of the outward sacrament of baptism is nearly always existential. It is the inward effect of baptism which is important. In his own case, of course, baptism signified a complete turnabout of his way of life. Instead of being a persecutor he became one of the perse-cuted (see Acts 8:1 and 9:2; 9:18-20).

Baptism was and is the rite of entry into the Church. It is clear from Acts of the Apostles that conversion was usually followed immediately by baptism (see Acts 8:36-39; 10:48). It was often the case that such baptisms took place out of doors, as indeed did the baptism of Jesus (cf. Matthew 3:13-17). When a convert accepted baptism this was sup-posed to signify a complete change of outlook, a move from the world of sin into the world of the righteousness of Christ (see Romans 6:10-11). Approximately three hundred years later the Emperor Constantine, the first Christian Roman emperor, postponed baptism as long as he decently could because he knew his way of life would have to change radically.

It is claimed by some Christians that infant baptism cannot have the full meaning of baptism in the way Paul describes it. There is an ongoing discussion as to whether adult baptism is more appropriate than infant baptism. Those who allow infant baptism, however, argue that the full effect of the promise made on behalf of the child comes later when the child is old enough to understand what the sacrament is about. It is probable that this difference of opinion will exist for the foreseeable future, but then, there are many differences of opinion within the Christian fold. These are very often legitimate differences of interpreta-tion and perhaps all of us need to develop a measure of tolerance about the way other people do things. Having said that, there may be some differences which are not acceptable by the majority of Christians. However, no one has yet managed to draw an exact line to show where "non-conformity" is not acceptable. Past attempts to do so have often been crude and have been followed up by severe repressive measures. This is hardly in the spirit of Christian love.

Paul sees a parallel between the death and resurrection of Jesus and the death of sin leading to new life in the baptised believer (6:5-8). It is as if the cross is imprinted through the soul. As every Christian knows, Christ defeated both death and sin on the cross. The resurrection which followed is also imprinted through the soul, and so the believer is taken into a new sphere of life. It is baptism which provides the key to this change. Baptism opens the door into the Church community and into the life of Christ.

Historically there have been differences of opinion as to how many sacraments there are. In early times many sacraments were listed. The mediaeval Church reduced the number to seven. The reformers of the sixteenth century reduced the number to two, that is, baptism and the Eucharist. Here again we have differences of opinion. However, there is no argument about the importance of baptism, nor about the centrality of the Eucharist. Perhaps, however, the early Church got it right in saying that there are many sacraments. Some people view the whole of life as sacramental. Certainly, baptism as Paul describes it should reach to every part of life. The life of the baptised Christian should perhaps be one long sacrament.

Bible readings

– Mark 1:1-13 (The baptism of Jesus)
– Acts 16:25-34 (Some converts are baptised)

XI
Judgement and the end of the world

1. The day of the Lord

For you yourselves know well that the day of the Lord will come like a thief in the night.

(I Thessalonians 5:2)

Paul seems to have expected the second coming of Christ within his own (Paul's) lifetime (see I Thessalonians 4:15), and he suggests in the verse quoted that the *parousia* will come when people least expect it (see above). Following the statement that "the day of the Lord will come like a thief in the night", Paul says further that when most people feel safe and secure it is then that sudden destruction will come upon them (v. 3). This could almost be from the Book of Amos. It was this prophet who first defined the day of the Lord as a day of judgement rather than as a day of rejoicing:

"Woe to you who desire the day of the Lord!
Why would you have the day of the Lord?
It is darkness and not light..." (Amos 5:18).

Amos goes on to say that the day of the Lord will happen unexpectedly, just as if a man was secure in his house and was leaning comfortably with his hand against the wall, when a "serpent bit him" (Amos 5:19).

Our Lord himself says, in a passage sometimes called the Little Apocalypse, " But of that day or that hour no one knows, not even the angels in heaven... take heed, watch; for you do not know when the time will come"

(Mark 13:32-33). The expression "that day" is usually taken to be equivalent to "the day of the Lord". In a similar context Luke quotes Jesus as saying, "...so will it be on the day when the Son of man is revealed. On that day, let him who is on the housetop, with his goods in the house, not come down to take them away..." (Luke 17:30). Paul writes elsewhere of "the day of Christ", hoping that when that day arrives he will not have lived his life in vain (Philippians 2:16).

Yet, in Thessalonians, following the verse under discussion, Paul is encouraging about the day of the Lord. He suggests to the congregation at Thessalonica: "But you are not in darkness, brethren, for that day to surprise you like a thief. For you are all sons of light and sons of the day; for we are not of the night or of darkness. So then let us not sleep, as others do, but let us keep awake and be sober" (5:4-6). This means that Christians should never relax their vigilance but should wear the armour of faith, hope and love (v. 8).

Belief in the day of the Lord was part of what is sometimes called the eschatological expectation, that is a belief in certain events associated with the "last things", meaning that one day history will achieve its divinely planned objective. A time of tribulation and the appearance of the anti-Christ are supposed to precede the parousia (I John 2:18; Revelation 15:1,7 and 16:17-19). At the end of the rule of anti-Christ Christ will return (see Acts 1:11; Matthew 24:3,27). Christ, of course, is already reigning, but his power will be made manifest to all (I Corinthians 1:7; II Thessalonians 1:7-8). The resurrection of the dead will happen when Christ appears (I Thessalonians 4:16) and the redeemed will enjoy a blessed life (Colossians 1:12-13). Judgement for all people will also take place at the Second Coming (Acts 17:31). At that time the kingdom of God will be fully established for all to see, though some will not inherit the kingdom (I Corinthians 6:9).

The above is merely a brief sketch of some of the

factors which the Bible shows are part of the eschatological expectation. The full picture is much more complex and there are very many biblical citations which fill out the picture. It has to be remembered also that there are different interpretations of the day of the Lord and the future judgement. For us today, however, the warning Paul gives is just as valid as it was to the congregation at Thessalonica. There are moral principles of divine origin in the world and we ignore them at our peril. It was Friedrich von Schiller who said, "The world's history is the world's judgement" (Die Weltgeschichte ist das Weltgericht), and there is some truth in this statement. However, it is God's ultimate judgement on those who make history which is important, and that judgement will come to all of us, whether we are at the centre of the world's stage or whether we are in the wings.

Bible readings

– II Thessalonians 1:5-12 (The righteous judgement of God)
– I Corinthians 15:20-28 (Christ will put all his enemies under his feet)

2. God's plan for the fullness of time

For he has made known to us in all wisdom and insight the mystery of his will, according to his purpose which he set forth in Christ as a plan for the fullness of time, to unite all things in him, things in heaven and things on earth.

(Ephesians 1:9-10)

Paul refers to the special insights and wisdom which Christians have through God's revelation of himself and his purposes. Before the time of the full revelation in the Incarnation, and especially before the beginning of the

201

biblical revelation to the Chosen people, the world was in comparative ignorance. True, from the beauty and harmony of nature, people could work out that there might well be a creator God. But until God revealed himself, first to the Jewish patriarchs and then to the prophets, people had no sure knowledge of God's true nature. Of course, people had previously built religious systems and had tried to postulate what God (or gods) might be like, but there is a limit to how much we can discover about the divine mystery by ourselves. Only with the beginning and fulfilment of God's own revelation were people able to come to a more realistic assessment of what God is like.

Not only has God revealed himself as a God of love, but he has also given guidelines relating to his will for the world and to his plan for "the fullness of time". God's will is revealed in the gospel of salvation (v. 13). This is personal. It is the gospel of your salvation and with that goes a guarantee of "our inheritance" as children of God (vv. 5 and 14). The phrase "fullness of time" is a very meaningful expression in the original Greek. There are several words for time in Greek, but the one used here (*kairos*) describes a fixed or special time, an appointed time. The same phrase is ascribed to Jesus in Mark's Gospel to indicate that a special time was imminent:

"The time is fulfilled, and the kingdom of God is at hand; repent and believe in the gospel" (Mark 1:15).

Indeed, an appropriate translation of the phrase in Paul's letter to Ephesus would be "the fulfilled time", which indicates an expected time for the fulfilment of God's will and purpose.

Paul sees God's ultimate purpose as the unity of all things in Christ, the binding together of "things in heaven and things on earth" (v. 10). This is not simply the earthly Church and the heavenly Church, for though the Church is God's special instrument, his purpose is for the whole of creation on earth and in heaven. As it says in the Lord's

Prayer, "Thy kingdom come, on earth as in heaven." This will happen at the *eschaton* (the end time) mentioned in the previous section. Indeed, the phrase "the fullness of time" can almost be equated with the idea of "the day of the Lord" already discussed.

How realistic is this eschatological hope? Is it "pie in the sky" or does it have some foundation in fact? There are facts, of course, such as the fact that Jesus was a historical person and that he was condemned to death by Pontius Pilate. The saints of the Christian tradition are also mostly historical personages. However, for the most part we are relying in our religion upon other ways of knowing things. Intuition and faith are just as important as scientific or historical investigation. And as Paul himself says, "If for this life only we have hoped in Christ, we are of all men most to be pitied" (I Corinthians 15:19). To disbelieve the gospel according to Paul and others, we have to ignore their commitment and testimony. However, the Christian faith does not depend entirely on the witness of others. It is a faith to be tested and tried by each individual. The challenge surely is to try the relationship with Christ. Very few people have tried it and found it wanting. Therefore, if Christ is real in our experience we also have a very real hope in the resurrection and the power of God's kingdom, both now and at the end of time.

Isaac Watts was conscious of earthly time's limitations when he wrote:

"A thousand ages in thy sight
Are like an evening gone;
Short as the watch that ends the night
Before the rising sun."

But the "watch that ends the night" brings the resurrection which takes us into God's time, into the "fullness of time" of which Paul speaks.

- I Corinthians 2:6-9 (The hidden wisdom of God)
- Colossians 4:2-6 (Making the most of time)

3. God is not mocked

Do not be deceived: God is not mocked, for whatever a man sows, that he will also reap. For he who sows to his own flesh will from the flesh reap corruption; but he who sows to the Spirit will from the Spirit reap eternal life.

(Galatians 6:7-8)

Paul's thought here and in the preceding verses is very much one of the Christian accepting responsibility for his (or her) own life and his own actions (see especially v. 5). At the same time the Christian ought to try to help those who have slipped up in some way (v. 1). Further, the sharing of all the good things one has with others is also high on Paul's list (v. 6). However, the verses under discussion (vv. 7-8) are about receiving our just deserts in the moral sense. Whatever we sow, that will we also reap. This is certainly true for the farmer. If he sows potatoes he is not going to reap barley. The parallel is that if a person sows goodness he will reap a harvest of goodness and conversely, if he sows evil, he will reap evil consequences for himself.

There is an obvious parallel with the curse and blessing in the Book of Deuteronomy:

"And if you obey the voice of the Lord your God, being careful to do all his commandments... all these blessings shall come upon you..."

(Deuteronomy 28:1-2)

"But if you will not obey the voice of the Lord your God... then all these curses shall come upon you..."

(Deuteronomy 28:15)

Of course, in Deuteronomy the blessing and the curse are outlined in very practical, this world terms. The blessing will bring good harvests, victory over enemies and many children. The curse will bring poor harvests, defeat by enemies, illness and barrenness (Deuteronomy 28).

Paul, however, implies that the results of good or bad behaviour are spiritual, rather than physical. The key words are "eternal life". Those who "sow to the Spirit" will reap eternal life, while those who sow to their own flesh (i.e. live sinfully) will "reap corruption". The latter phrase is somewhat ambiguous, but Paul may mean that the spirits of determined and unrepentant sinners will be as corrupt as their bodies. It is true, of course, that a dissolute life leaves its mark on the face and body, as well as on the soul. To that extent Paul would no doubt agree with the writer of the Book of Deuteronomy. In other words, the kind of life we lead morally has both short term effects in this life and long term effects through into the next life. Despite any trials that may come to us during our lives, if we are living with Christ and we are at least trying to be good in the moral sense, then a deep inner serenity is possible in even the most disastrous circumstances. On the other hand, if we have no faith and if we abandon any attempt to be loving and caring, living only for ourselves, then we have no deep well of comfort within us. The result is deep unhappiness.

As Paul says, God will not be deceived by any facade we may raise to hide our true selves. If we pray hypocritically and go to church with no intention of taking our responsibilities seriously, that would be a case of "mocking God"; but God is not mocked – he will allow our sins to find us, and find us they most surely do in one way or another.

It is puzzling, of course, when some people seem not to care about moral standards or loving others, and yet appear to lead prosperous lives. This seems to reverse the curse of the Book of Deuteronomy. This is a problem that was recognised by other Old Testament writers, for example, Job and the Preacher (the author of Ecclesiastes). How-

ever, both Paul and the Book of Deuteronomy are ultimately right. There is a moral law within the universe and
it is inexorable. The consequences of our behaviour will be
faced sooner or later, in this life or the next. Those who
appear to be escaping the consequences of absolute and
utter selfishness, unenlightened by even a glimmer of love,
will eventually meet their come-uppance.

Bible readings

- II Corinthians 9:6-9 (Sowing bountifully)
- I Corinthians 6:9-11 (The unrighteous will not inherit
  the kingdom of God)

4. Condemnation or acquittal?

*Then as one man's trespass led to condemnation for all
men, so one man's act of righteousness leads to acquittal
and life for all men. For as by one man's disobedience
many were made sinners, so by one man's obedience many
will be made righteous. Law came in, to increase the trespass; but where sin increased, grace abounded all the
more, so that, as sin reigned in death, grace also might
reign through righteousness to eternal life through Jesus
Christ our Lord.*

(Romans 5:18-21)

The trespass of the one man refers to the Fall of Man
epitomised in the story of Adam (see preceding verses in
Romans 5:12-14 and Genesis 2-3). It would be impossible
to say whether Paul believed that Adam was a historical
person. He would be aware, however, that the word "Adam"
is simply the Hebrew word for "man" so he would readily
accept Adam as the typical first human being.

It is interesting that the early chapters of the Bible
describe the origin of human sin when one of the main

themes of the whole Bible is the redemption of humanity from its sinful state. The writer of the Genesis story can hardly have been aware that Christ, the incarnate Son of God, was to come later. It is difficult not to conclude, however, that God's inspiration worked through the Fall story in order to prepare the way for the revelations of the New Testament.

The story of the Fall explains the existence of sin in the world. The life of Christ explains how sin has been defeated. This is the essence of Paul's thought: that through one man, Adam, sin was born; and through one man, Christ, sin was overcome. While this is a universal story which applies to all human beings throughout history, it is also the individual story of every man or every woman. Each of us becomes conscious of temptation and sin as we grow older; and those who are fortunate hear the preaching of the gospel of redemption through Christ. What happens to those who have no opportunity to hear the gospel, either because they lived before Christ or because they did not have the opportunity during their lives? Only God knows, but it is a fair assumption that the God who is love will take all things into account. This principle must apply to all of us. Only God knows fully the various pressures which have worked upon each human being. We would all recognise that sometimes pressures beyond our control persuade us to do things against our better judgement. Having said that, we also know that we sometimes have nobody to blame but ourselves for our failings. That will surely also be taken into account.

However, the beauty and wonder of the gospel of redemption through Christ is that sins are forgiven. As Paul says, "...where sin increased, grace abounded all the more..." Of course, in the first verse of the next chapter (6:1) he gives a stern warning against any presumption that we should deliberately continue in sin because we know that grace is available. If we have died to sin, then we should not still be living in our former sinful state (see 6:2).

Yet again, Paul speaks of the promise of eternal life (5:21). Not only has the one righteous man, Christ, conquered sin, he has also conquered death. Christ is the living Lord and through him we are invited to a continuing life beyond this one. That is the plain meaning of the text and it is the heart of the Christian faith, that Christ died for our sins and rose again from the dead, taking us with him both metaphorically within our growing consciousness, and literally to the glory of God's eternal kingdom. To Paul, the Easter message is double sided. We experience the resurrection now as we grow through and out of our sinful state; and we shall experience the full resurrection at some time after death, in God's time. The joy and glory of this double message is expressed well by St John of Damascus (translated by J.M. Neale):

> "The day of Resurrection!
> Earth tell it out abroad;
> The Passover of gladness,
> The Passover of God!
> From death to life eternal,
> From earth unto the sky,
> Our God hath brought us over
> With hymns of victory.
>
> "Our hearts be pure from evil,
> That we may see aright
> The Lord in rays eternal
> Of resurrection light..."

Bible readings

- I Corinthians 15:50-54 (What is raised is imperishable)
- Acts 13:32-39 (Paul preaches the resurrection)

5. Judge of the living and the dead

I charge you in the presence of God and of Christ Jesus who is to judge the living and the dead, and by his appearing and his kingdom: preach the word, be urgent in season and out of season, convince, rebuke, and exhort, be unfailing in patience and in teaching.

(II Timothy 4:1-2)

Paul's charge to Timothy is a very solemn one. The promise that Christ will come again "to judge the living and the dead" is a stark reminder that the task of a Christian leader is to use all legitimate means to prepare his flock for the day of the Lord. Those still alive at the time of Christ's appearing will be judged alongside those who have previously died. In Acts of the Apostles, Peter is recorded as having made a similar statement:

"And he (Christ) commanded us to preach to the people, and to testify that he is the one ordained by God to be judge of the living and the dead"

(Acts 10:42; cf. I Peter 4:5)

Paul is aware of the dangers and temptations that beset people. He warns of those who do not listen to the truth and "wander into myths" (II Timothy 4:4). Even in modern times people are tempted to follow revivals of nature myths or astrological fallacies. The advice Paul gives to Timothy is: "...always be steady, endure suffering, do the work of an evangelist, fulfil your ministry" (v. 5). This is good advice for Christian ministers in any age.

On the question of the Day of Judgement, the Bible sometimes promises that Christ will be the judge, as in the text quoted above, though some texts say that God will be the judge (see Acts 17:31; Hebrews 12:23). Paul himself talks of both the judgement seat of God (Romans 14:10) and the judgement seat of Christ (II Corinthians 5:10). There is no real contradiction here because Christ is within the Godhead.

Paul's thoughts about judgement are scattered here and there in his letters, which is not surprising. He was not, after all, writing a treatise about God's judgement. He does say in the letter to the Romans that those who have not lived under the law of Moses will be judged outside that law and that those who have lived under Mosaic law will be judged according to that law (Romans 2:12). Whichever category people come under, if they have deliberately and persistently followed unrighteousness, they will be condemned (Romans 2:6-8). With such a serious view of the final judgement, it is easy to see why Paul felt the need to give such a strong exhortation to Timothy.

However, Paul is always careful to point out that God has made possible the salvation of humankind by the atoning work of Christ upon the cross (see earlier in II Timothy at 2:10-13). Paul's teaching about salvation and justification is spelled out more clearly elsewhere. Justification is the antithesis of judgement. This justification is already at work in the heart of the believer through faith in Christ (see especially Romans 3:21-26; 5:1; 8:33,34). Fortunately it is Christ "who was raised from the dead, who is at the right hand of God, who indeed intercedes for us" (Romans 8:34).

At the same time, Paul makes it clear that we shall all appear before the judgement seat of Christ (II Corinthians 5:10). This is an awesome prospect for all of us. There is no escape from this truth of the final judgement. However, those who have lived daily with Christ should not be afraid of the final judgement, for their lives and their actions have been open to God. Paul places a great emphasis on love (see especially I Corinthians 13). The more our hearts are filled with the love of Christ, then the less room there is for sin. The inspired words of John Newton are very helpful in this respect:

"How sweet the name of Jesus sounds
In a believers ear!
It soothes his sorrows, heals his wounds,
And drives away his fear.

"It makes the wounded spirit whole,
And calms the troubled breast;
'Tis manna to the hungry soul,
And to the weary rest."

Bible readings

- II Thessalonians 1:5-12 (The righteous judgement of God)
- Romans 14:10-12 (We shall all stand before the judgement seat of God)

6. A judgement of fire

Now if anyone builds on the foundation with gold, silver, precious stones, wood, hay, straw – each man's work will become manifest; for the day will disclose it, because it will be revealed with fire, and the fire will test what sort of work each one has done. If the work any man has built on the foundation survives, he will receive a reward. If any man's work is burned up, he will suffer loss, though he himself will be saved, but only as through fire.

(I Corinthians 3:12-15)

This comparison with the building of a house inevitably reminds us of our Lord's parable of the two house builders in the Sermon on the Mount (see Matthew 7:24-27). As in the parable of Jesus, Paul also uses the comparison of the wise man and the foolish man (I Corinthians 3:18). The occasion for the discussion is the rivalry between different evangelists. Paul says that such rivalry is out of place because "no other foundation can anyone lay than that which is laid, which is Jesus Christ" (v. 11).

This thought leads Paul on to say that we shall all be judged according to the kind of building we have produced. Some buildings are of lasting materials whereas others are of easily combustible materials. The Day (i.e. the day of the Lord or the Day of Judgement) will reveal what kind of materials each of our houses is made of. The fire of God's judgement will sweep through each house. Only if we have built our houses with good materials will they survive. Those who have tried to live good lives in the light of Christ will find they still have a house. Those who have led deliberately sinful lives will find themselves homeless. This could mean they will find no place to live in heaven. However, the fire is also a purifying agent and even those whose houses have not survived may be saved (v. 15).

The idea of the fire of judgement appears in several places in the Bible. For example, when John the Baptist described the coming of Christ he prophesied that there would be a baptism of the Holy Spirit and of fire. Of course, the fire of the Holy Spirit is creative and purifying in its effects. However, the winnowing fork wielded by Christ will sort out the grain from the chaff, and the chaff will "burn with unquenchable fire" (see Matthew 3:11-12).

Paul uses the image of fire elsewhere to describe the divine judgement. This will come "...when the Lord Jesus is revealed from heaven with his mighty angels in flaming fire, inflicting vengeance upon those who do not know God and upon those who do not obey the gospel of our Lord Jesus" (II Thessalonians 1:7-8). Those "who do not know God" are presumably those who live with supreme selfishness, rather than those who have not had the opportunity to hear the gospel. In a way, a person can know God without being acquainted with him, because to live lovingly is to know God's ways. In that sense, unbelievers can know God.

The person who is fortunate enough to know God through Christ does, however, have a great responsibility. He (or she) knows what God expects from each of us. To love God and our neighbour is at the heart of worship and Christian ethics. Those who sincerely try to follow those principles are building with lasting materials which will not be quenched by the fire of judgement. On the other hand, those who have met the love of Christ and have then abandoned his love are in the worst position of all. They have virtually made themselves homeless by deliberate choice.

To be sure, Jesus himself tells us: "In my Father's house there are many rooms; if it were not so, would I have told you that I go to prepare a place for you?" (John 14:2). This is the Christian hope, that we go eventually to live in one of the many rooms of heaven. There our Lord himself will welcome us and he will be with us on the Day of Judgement.

Bible readings

- II Corinthians 5:6-10 (We must all appear before the judgement seat of Christ)
- Romans 2:6-8 (He will render to every man according to his works)

7. The wages of sin

For the wages of sin is death, but the free gift of God is eternal life in Christ Jesus our Lord.

(Romans 6:23)

This verse comes at the end of a discussion about sin and obedience, about death and life, about repentance and renewal. Paul uses the idea of death in several ways. Of course, there is the literal sense in which we die at the end of our earthly lives and then by God's grace partake of eternal life (6:9). He also uses the idea symbolically to refer to the death of sin and our subsequent self renewal (6:4). However, in the verse under consideration he seems to be referring to something different. To continue in sin leads to death or, as Paul puts it, "The wages of sin is

213

death..." (v. 23). Now it is obvious that we all die anyway, so what does Paul mean? He must surely refer to a cessation of any kind of life, even after the death of the physical body. In other words, this is the opposite of eternal life with Christ. Unrepentant sinners are consigned to a second death. Whether this is symbolic for life in hell or whether Paul means that the soul fades into nothingness is not clear.

In either case the prospect is a fearful one. This means being separated from the love of God; but it is a self motivated separation. It may be assumed that God would not give up a soul to death easily, so it may be that each of us is offered several opportunities to change, if not in this life, then beyond the grave. Those who refuse to turn to love and persist in absolute selfishness will then enter an existence so meaningless that it is equivalent to another death. This view is not without its difficulties. It can hardly be supposed that God created us and offered us the further development of eternal life, only for some souls to be destined in his deliberations not to reach that state of bliss. However, in that creative process God has given each of us freedom of choice. The consequence then is that those who choose the "wages of sin" do so in their given freedom.

Another difficulty is whether God's love is ultimately resistible. Alongside that it may be asked if God's will is ultimately deniable? These questions are impossible for us to answer. We may, however, postulate that God invites people to grace and does not force people to accept his love. Perhaps this invitation is permanently open, even to those in the state of the second death which is a version of hell. As Paul says elsewhere, "Love never ends" (I Corinthians 13:8). God is love and God is eternal, so his love surely shines without ceasing through the whole of all the dimensions he has created. God is also all powerful so all things are possible with him. Here we come face to face with a mystery. Perhaps the best we can do is to pray in our state of partial knowledge (cf. I Corinthians 13:12) for all souls, wherever they may be, and to commend them and ourselves to God's merciful care.

In the text under discussion Paul balances his words carefully. Even though "The wages of sin is death...", it is also true that "the free gift of God is eternal life in Christ Jesus our Lord." God gives us so much: life and breath, an incredibly beautiful universe in which to live, a love that is never-ending, a promise of further joys to come after this life is ended. Those who do not know this gospel are to be pitied. The nature of eternal life is not spelled out by Paul or anyone else. Reason suggests, however, that if this life is so wonderful at its best, in spite of the multitude of pains and disasters that may strike any of us, how much more wonderful will be the life to come. Dimensions unimaginable await us. The love of Christ awaits us. As Paul himself says, "My desire is to depart and be with Christ, for that is far better" (Philippians 1:23). Separation from a loved one who dies is naturally extremely painful, but if that loved one is with Christ, then our mourning is in some sense for ourselves and our own bereavement. The faith we learn from Paul, however, shows us that such separations are but temporary. God's promise of eternal life through Christ is not an empty one. As Paul says very powerfully elsewhere:

"Death is swallowed up in victory.
O Death, where is thy victory?
O death, where is thy sting?"

(I Corinthians 15:54-55;
Cf. Isaiah 25:8 and Hosea 13:14)

Bible readings

- II Corinthians 5:1-5 (We long to put on our heavenly dwelling)
- Romans 8:31-39 (Nothing can separate us from the love of Christ)

XII
Final prayers

1. A blessing

The grace of the Lord Jesus Christ and the love of God and the fellowship of the Holy Spirit be with you all.

(II Corinthians 13:14)

2. Glory be to God for evermore

Now to him who is able to strengthen you according to my gospel and the preaching of Jesus Christ, according to the revelation of the mystery which was kept secret for long ages but is now disclosed and through the prophetic writings is made known to all nations, according to the command of the eternal God, to bring about the obedience of faith – to the only wise God be glory for evermore through Jesus Christ! Amen.

(Romans 16:25-27)

NOTE: The Second Letter of Peter contains an interesting comment about St Paul's letters:

"And count the forbearance of our Lord as salvation. So also our beloved brother Paul wrote to you according to the wisdom given him, speaking of this as he does in all his letters. There are some things in them hard to understand, which the ignorant and the unstable twist to their own destruction, as they do other scriptures" (II Peter 3:15-16).

It is true of course that parts of St Paul's letters are hard to understand, but sincere efforts to understand Paul's writings are always worthwhile. He is a great Christian theologian and without his work we should not be able to understand fully the Incarnation of Christ and God's wonderful revelation through his Son. Paul was a man touched by God and his writings are indeed an important part of the divine revelation.

by the same author

THE TREASURES OF JESUS

This book is a thoughtful commentary about the Sermon on the Mount, which is a collection of the sayings of Jesus of Nazareth to be found in Matthew's Gospel (Chapters 5-7). The Sermon is one the world's most important documents because it records the sayings of a person who, at the very least, was a great religious teacher. Christians, of course, believe that Jesus was more than that, in fact, that he was the Son of God.

The author comments on the text, drawing out its meaning, but also discuss the implications of the sayings of Jesus for today. At the end of each section there are three suggested readings from other parts of the Bible. Each set of readings illuminates one of the sayings of Jesus and they are specially chosen to take up the same theme. Also, there is an appropriate prayer after each section.

The book can be used by individuals to learn more about the implications of what Jesus said in his Sermon. They will be able then to meditate on the sayings. At the same time, the material is suitable for study groups and certainly the sayings, together with the author's comments, do stimulate discussion.

Alan Robinson studied theology at New College, University of Edinburgh. He was formerly Principal Lecturer in Theology and Religious Studies at the Derbyshire College of Higher Education (now the University of Derby). He has previously published children's books, theological articles and poetry.

ISBN 085439 466 4 – 142 pages

ST PAULS